Real World Research

Small-Scale Social Survey Methods

Also available from Continuum

Real World Research series

Case Study Research Methods, Bill Gillham
The Research Interview, Bill Gillham
Observation Techniques, Bill Gillham
Developing a Questionnaire 2nd Edition, Bill Gillham

Also available

Questionnaire Design, Interviewing and Attitude Measurement,
   A. N. Oppenheim

Small-Scale Social Survey Methods

Bill Gillham

Real World Research

continuum

Continuum International Publishing Group
The Tower Building   80 Maiden Lane, Suite 704
11 York Road   New York, NY 10038
London SE1 7NX

www.continuumbooks.com

British Library Cataloguing-in-Publication Data
A catalogue record for this book is available from the British Library.
ISBN: 9780826496300 (paperback)

Library of Congress Cataloging-in-Publication Data
Gillham, Bill.
Small-scale social survey methods / Bill Gillham.
p. cm.
ISBN-13: 978–0-8264–9630-0 (pbk.)
ISBN-10: 0–8264-9630-X (pbk.)
1. Social surveys–Methodology. I. Title.
HM538.G55 2007
300.72'3–dc22   2007026663

Typeset by Data Standards Ltd, Frome, Somerset

Contents

List of Figures and Tables

Figures

Tables

Series Foreword

The success of the first books in this series was encouraging but not entirely surprising. Research is a practical activity and few methods texts, even relatively advanced ones, are sufficiently practical at the level of useable detail. And those hefty, apparently comprehensive 'introductory' tomes – dispiriting to students – are usually only adequate for writing exam answers: hardly an end in itself.

A further limitation of existing texts is that they tend to present a prescription impossible within the constraints of a modest research project in a real-world setting. Or, indeed, in anything less than an ideal world. Like any other engagement with reality, research is often a matter of making the best compromise that nonetheless preserves the essential values of a disciplined investigation.

Bill Gillham

Acknowledgements

I am indebted to Dr Josephine Webb for her very detailed commentary on a late draft of the text; Clare Cannon for her patience and word-processing skills through several revisions; and my wife, Judith, for invaluable editorial help.

1

Social Surveys: Basic Issues

What is a social survey? At one level the question hardly needs asking. Surveys – of what people do and their opinions and preferences – are part of our daily experience. Walking along a crowded shopping street you are likely to be accosted by a market researcher ready with clipboard and instant friendliness. In the bank you may be handed a token to insert into one of a series of slots rating counter service from *excellent* to *unsatisfactory*. On a holiday flight you are often asked to fill in a questionnaire with a similar rating scale; and because we're captive, with nothing better to do, we usually complete them even if they don't allow us to say what we really think.

You don't need to be an expert to see that the quality (accuracy, usefulness) of these kinds of data is likely to be poor. In fact almost all survey data have limitations, even when the study is well planned and executed. Achieving a high standard can be expensive, requiring technical resources and specialist staff. But it is perfectly possible to carry out a small-scale survey just using your own resources which results in useful data of respectable quality, perhaps as part of a wider piece of research. This is where the present book comes in.

The nature of survey data

To understand the uses of surveys we need to ask: what kinds of data do they yield? Broadly speaking these are:

1. Basic facts about people (usually known as *subject descriptors*): age range, gender, occupational category, educational level, income range and so on.
2. What people *do* (their *behaviour*): what newspapers they buy, what television programmes they watch, how they travel to work: all the habits of their daily life.
3. What people's *opinions* are (judgements, preferences, intentions): which party they would vote for in an election, what they think of the primary medical care they receive or their local refuse recycling facilities and so on.

The data obtained under 2 and 3 can be subdivided to see if there are any differences according to the subject descriptors – by age, gender or occupational category, for example. This interesting area (which can lead to further research) is dealt with in Chapter 12.

One important characteristic of survey data is that they are the result of counting different answers, i.e. the data are *quantitative*: How many people say they would vote for the Labour Party? How many residents (a) regularly use the bottle banks? And (b) think they are conveniently sited?

So surveys can be quite good at answering *who?* and *what?* questions. What they are not good at is answering *why?* The point is emphasized because if we find significant differences (by gender, income level or whatever) in what people do or think, we can be tempted to infer an explanation particularly if it seems 'obvious', that most dangerous of terms. Here we are entering the territory of what people say and do actually *means* – the underlying reasons. This is the area of *qualitative* research: the most difficult and, in human terms, the most interesting.

Description versus explanation

Because survey data are largely quantitative (counting people and responses) they are easily subjected to statistical manipulation. The differing responses can be thought of as a *variable* (an attribute on which people vary). Such attributes can be combined to form *hypothetical constructs* but here we are on a slippery slope. Of course in everyday life we sometimes describe people as 'aggressive', 'anxious' or 'intelligent' – inferences from what they do or say. But aggression, anxiety and intelligence are hypothetical constructs even though the terms are so common as to seem 'real'. Here we are into the philosophical sphere of *ontology* which is concerned with the nature of the existence of concepts like these; the fact that we have a 'name' for something doesn't mean it exists as an entity.

Survey data, expressed as variables, can be used to define or assert the existence of such constructs; for instance, to take examples from a recent text on the subject (Punch 2003), self-esteem, alienation and social cohesion. The *existence* of these notions or constructs can be bolstered psychometrically by including a number of slightly different questions (and responses) on which people vary, i.e. score more or less differently. In that way it is possible to construct an entity and so assert its existence. Exactly the same thing is done in developing items for intelligence and personality tests. And because they produce variable results *(scores)* one could, for example, correlate the social class of schoolchildren and their 'alienation' from school. And that, unless critically interrogated, might then assume the character of explanation even though statistical correlation means nothing of the sort; and in any case the variable (alienation) may be an *artefact* (an artificial product) of the way the questionnaire and the items in it were constructed and scored.

These are difficult issues to deal with in a summary fashion but they are basic to our argument, so we'll make the attempt.

● Surveys are best used (most valid – accurate, meaningful) for gathering relatively straightforward information (personal details, behaviour, simple judgements and preferences of a non-abstract character).

- The interpretation of material beyond the descriptive level should proceed with caution and, when something apparently significant emerges, should involve follow-up exploratory interviews.
- The existence of apparently 'simple' constructs, such as levels of satisfaction, should be rooted in preliminary qualitative research (interviews, focus groups) so that items in a survey questionnaire have a basis other than the researcher's suppositions.
- The pursuit of relationships between variables should be carefully scrutinized both for the validity of all the variables involved but also for their interpretation (what does this apparent 'relationship' mean?).
- Conspicuous findings unearthed in this way should be the subject of further qualitative research to explore the meaning or character of the apparent relationship.

Reviewing a postgraduate student's research project a decade ago I concluded with the phrase: *too much metric, not enough meaning.* It is a common failing in social research.

Getting the wider picture

Nothing that has been written above should be taken as devaluing social surveys, rather that they should not be expected to do what they are not good at – explaining human behaviour and differences between people. However, researchers engaged in a qualitative study such as an in-depth interview-based project may be concerned as to how typical or 'representative' the individuals involved are of the group as a whole. These anxieties are unfounded if no empirical generalization is going to be claimed, i.e. if it is not being put forward as statistically representative of the larger group. 'Representativeness' in any case has two meanings:

1. *Quantitative representation:* when the sample is proportionately pro-rata to a group or population as a whole – what we usually understand when we ask whether a group is representative.
2. *Qualitative representation:* when the members of the sample are of the same *kind* as the wider group – for example, if we were researching teenage single mothers then older women or even teenagers in general would not be representative.

Procedures for constructing samples differ according to the purpose of the research: and there is a great variety. Sampling is an extensive topic with many specialist volumes devoted to it. It is also widely misunderstood. The next two chapters deal with different sampling techniques appropriate to small-scale research. But before that we should ask: Do you need to do a survey at all? That might seem a rather odd question in a book on the subject, but in research everything has to be justified – particularly the methods or tools you employ. Are they fit for purpose? And what is meant by 'purpose'?

Research is about getting answers to questions, methods the means of doing so. Novice researchers often specify the method before they have clarified their purpose. And surveys are often selected mainly, it seems, because of the appeal of questionnaires – a 'quick fix' to obtain a lot of data – with the issues of data quality (modest, at best) and suitability being barely considered.

There are, of course, other ways of carrying out surveys than using questionnaire's; Chapter 9 deals with structured interviews, either face-to-face or by telephone. But whatever research topic is in mind the choice is determined by:

- what the researcher wants to find out;
- which instruments are most likely to provide data of suitable quality;
- what time and other resources are available.

For the lone researcher the choice is often between quantity and quality: we shall be arguing throughout that the latter should be the primary consideration; and that a small-scale survey, intensive in character, is more likely to provide significant data and indicate the probable useful content for a larger-scale survey.

A practical example

Suppose your research focus is the exploration of social factors that support the independent living of older people: an area where it is easy to make assumptions about what might be important. It is on that basis and not much more that many survey questionnaires are constructed; such assumptions may set you wrong from the start.

Questionnaires, which are normally highly structured instruments, are predicated on the supposition that you know what you want to find out. The necessary preparation for a survey questionnaire involves either relatively *unstructured interviews* with individuals from the target group, or *focus groups* similarly composed (see Chapter 5).

An unstructured interview is one where the researcher raises the topics and follows up the interviewees' responses – wherever they are going. You don't know what you are going to find. Both the areas of importance and what underpins them may be quite unexpected. A focus group operates in a similar way.

Suppose a topic that comes up is access to the state pension. In the UK this can be paid either by electronic bank transfer or by going to a post office with a payment card to draw cash. For many of us the latter arrangement would be cumbersome and inconvenient, compared to the choice of telephone and online banking for most payments, easy access to free ATMs for cash and, of course, usually making purchases by card.

However, for many pensioners (often among the poorest in our society) not all these options are available and the detail of some of the problems they experience or profess may come as a surprise. For example:

- that they don't have a bank account;
- that they don't have a telephone let alone a computer;
- that the trip to the post office is an 'occasion' for them, perhaps their only social contact in a day;
- that they prefer 'real' money, i.e. cash;
- that they feel they manage their money better when it's in cash;
- that they are anxious their local post office may close or lose the card account, when the post office provides them with access to other services and informed advice.

Assuming that you could construct a questionnaire that would tap into all these dimensions, would such a group be likely to complete it?

Quite often in small-scale survey work you come to see that a self-administered questionnaire is both impractical and unsatisfactory.

Perhaps the survey data already exist?

If we are a much surveyed society it has to be said that much of the information gathered can be very useful to a researcher. In the UK such publications as the *British Crime Survey* and the *General Household Survey* – carried out and updated periodically – give a wealth of detail which may provide the framework for a more focused study (see Office of National Statistics website www. statistics.gov.uk). Official statistics on births, marriages and deaths (including causes), usually related to social indices of one kind or another (age group, marital status, social class) are another rich source. The main sources of such publicly available information in the UK are listed in the *General Household Survey* (ONS 2006).

Unpublished statistical data can also provide the raw material for survey analysis. Company records of employees (educational attainments, disability status, absence patterns and so on) may enable you to short-cut your investigation or provide pointers for further research. School, college and university records, those in hospital and general practice – carefully regulated – are other sources. Once you know what you're looking for you can often track down a contributory source.

There are two problems here: *access* and *confidentiality*. Increased public and professional sensitivity, related legislation and the ethical screening of research projects mean that this is not as easy as it first seems, and perhaps impossible. Even obtaining a list of names and contact details from which to take a sample may prove difficult. Researchers inhabit a real world with its political realities. The well-meaning researcher can cause problems for others; which is why you may encounter a cautious response.

2

Sampling: Probability or Random Methods

What do we mean by 'sampling'? The answer is a common sense one: in a restaurant we may sample the dish that is put in front of us, and on the basis of that forkful we decide whether or not we like it. In other words we make an *estimate* of the whole from the small part (or sample).

Similarly, in social surveys, that is what sampling is about: estimating the whole from the part. Of course the sample may be misleading: the first taste of our food may be better than the experience of the whole. In a large group of people (usually described as a *population*) one relatively small sample will not be exactly characteristic. This difference is known as *sampling error*: it is obvious that a fraction of a population will not be precisely the same as the group as a whole. Sampling procedures attempt to minimize this error and with random or probability sampling (see below) the size of the error can be estimated, yielding what are known as *confidence limits*.

Why sample?

Again the answer is a common sense one. If the group is large, say all the undergraduates in a major university, or the entire adult population of the UK, the cost of a complete survey, like the national census that takes place each decade, would be astronomical. In any case and for most purposes a much smaller number, properly sampled, will give an estimate with an acceptable degree of error. The emphasis has to be on the phrase 'properly sampled'. Some methods are certainly better than others. What we have to distance ourselves from are the media-type surveys where the 'sample', whether small or large, is collected in such a way that the claims made for it are nonsense (e.g. two-thirds of voters believe that . . .) based on people's emails or calls to a TV programme or internet site, i.e. self-selected. On top of this the framing of questions may 'lead' the responses and so further invalidate the 'findings'.

The use of percentages can also be a confounding factor, particularly where different groups of different sizes are concerned. A colleague once told me that in the previous year murders of women had increased by 10 per cent and murders of men by only 5 per cent. The *actual* numerical increase was greater for men because men are murdered much more often than women. So if a survey reported, for example, that 35 per cent of black teenagers compared to 20 per cent of white teenagers admitted to regularly carrying a knife, without our knowing the actual numbers involved (and how comparable they were) it would be quite meaningless.

To revert to the issue of sample size: with large groups, and limited resources, sampling is the only sensible procedure. But what if the group is small in the first place? For example, teachers of classical languages in state schools or, from my own experience, female Muslim students in art schools. These groups are so small that you can't afford to lose any – so, if possible, you should survey all of them.

As an individual researcher you commonly find yourself in an in-between situation. Say, for instance, that your research interest is the career ambitions of secondary school students within one particular school of 2,000. You decide that a short structured interview (see Chapter 9) lasting about 10 minutes with each student would be a sufficiently sensitive instrument and that a 10 per cent sample (200 students) would be feasible in terms of your time, including an allowance for some transcription, analysis and so on. How would you set about it? In this instance there are three main options: *random* or *probability* sampling; *systematic* sampling; and *stratified* sampling. In this example, since career ambitions change as children get older, you might opt for the last (sampling at different age levels or *strata*). We'll deal with all these variants in turn.

What is meant by random or probability sampling?

In this context 'random' and 'probability' mean the same thing: the latter term is now preferred because 'random' has a common-usage meaning which can cause confusion. When I have asked students how they chose the people they've included in a survey the reply is often: 'Oh, I just chose them at random'. By which they meant those who were available or came to hand: that kind of unsystematic approach is called *convenience* sampling (see p. 18–19).

To devise a probability sample you first need a list of *all* the people from which the sample is to be drawn. This is known as the *sampling frame*. Each person is then assigned a number: in the case of the secondary school students mentioned earlier, from 0001 to 2000. (You'll see why the numbers are in this format in a moment.)

Until computers came into general use, generating the numbers for a random sample involved using a random numbers table (to be found in the appendices of most statistics textbooks except for the more recent: see Table 2.1 for an example). I still find them useful for teaching purposes.

Each digit is determined randomly, i.e. it bears no relation to the one before or after. The digits are grouped in pairs so that your eye doesn't get lost: the groups have no other significance. To derive your sample of 200 students you proceed as follows:

Table 2.1   Excerpt from a random numbers table (Robson 1973)

66 67 40 67 14	64 05 71 95 86	11 05 65 09 68	76 83 20 37 90	57 16 00 11 66
14 90 84 45 11	75 73 88 05 90	52 27 41 14 86	22 98 12 22 08	07 52 74 95 80
68 05 51 18 00	33 96 02 75 19	07 60 62 93 55	59 33 82 43 90	49 37 38 44 59
20 46 78 73 90	97 51 40 14 02	04 02 33 31 08	39 54 16 49 36	47 95 93 13 30
64 19 58 97 79	15 06 15 93 20	01 90 10 75 06	40 78 78 89 62	02 67 74 87 33

1. Determine a starting point. If you haven't used the table
   before there is no harm in starting on the first line. But you *can*
   start anywhere. It is sometimes suggested that you should close
   your eyes and point blind – and start from where your finger
   has descended. It is possible to be too obsessional about this.
2. Break up the digits into groups of four horizontally by putting
   a line down between them; simply delete the two ungrouped
   digits at the end of the row.

Table 2.2 The same random digits in groups of four

66 67	40 67	14 64	05 71	95 86	11 05	65 09	68 76	83 20	37 90	57 16	00 11	66
14 90	84 45	11 75	73 88	05 90	52 27	41 14	86 22	98 12	22 08	07 52	74 95	80
68 05	51 18	00 33	96 02	75 19	07 60	62 93	55 59	33 82	43 90	49 37	38 44	59
20 46	78 73	78 73	51 40	14 02	04 02	33 31	08 39	54 16	49 36	47 95	93 13	30
64 19	58 97	58 97	06 15	93 20	01 90	10 75	06 40	78 78	89 62	02 67	74 87	33

3. Delete any numbers, which are more than 2,000 (the highest
   number in our sampling frame) or where the same number
   occurs more than once (simply delete these repetitions).

Table 2.3 The same groups of four with numbers above 2,000 deleted

~~66 67~~	~~40 67~~	14 64	05 71	~~95 86~~	11 05	~~65 09~~	~~68 76~~	~~83 20~~	~~37 90~~	~~57 16~~	00 11	~~66~~
14 90	~~84 45~~	11 75	~~73 88~~	05 90	~~52 27~~	~~41 14~~	~~86 22~~	~~98 12~~	~~22 08~~	07 52	~~74 95~~	~~80~~
~~68 05~~	~~51 18~~	00 33	~~96 02~~	~~75 19~~	07 60	~~62 93~~	~~55 59~~	~~33 82~~	~~43 90~~	49 37	~~38 44~~	~~59~~
~~20 46~~	~~78 73~~	~~78 73~~	~~51 40~~	14 02	04 02	~~33 31~~	08 39	~~54 16~~	~~49 36~~	~~47 95~~	~~93 13~~	~~30~~
~~64 19~~	~~58 97~~	~~58 97~~	06 15	~~93 20~~	01 90	10 75	06 40	~~78 78~~	~~89 62~~	02 67	~~74 87~~	~~33~~

4. Continue until you have the necessary sample of 200 from
   numbers up to 2,000.

5. Put them in numerical order, e.g.

0011
0033
0190
0267
0402
0571
0590
0615
0640
0752
0760
0839
1075
1105
1175
1402
1464
1490

and then identify them in your sampling frame. As you carry out the exercise the range will fill out but, at the moment, there appear to be 'gaps', e.g. nothing over 1,500, but this is what randomness means: it is not evenly spaced.

Deriving a sample in this way is straightforward: in the example quoted it would take no more than 45 minutes. You can, of course, generate random numbers using standard software. In *Excel*, for example, to generate a random number between **a** and **b** (the two limits of the number range) you simply type RAND( )* (b−a)+a into a cell on your spreadsheet and repeat until you have your sample. But for the researcher carrying out a small-scale study the manual procedure described may be all that is necessary. Whatever the sample size it is a relatively easy matter to calculate the *standard error of measurement* (see Moser and Kalton 1986, p. 66). Explaining this to others is another matter not least because they will understand 'sampling error' in a different way.

13

At the level of individual students selected you may find it hard to convince, for example, teachers from whose class a small number of children are identified that there is an objective process. As a primary school teacher once said to me: 'Of course, you would pick the worst three in my class'. I made some feeble excuse: it wasn't the time or place for a lecture on probability theory.

Limitations of probability sampling

Despite its ideal characteristics, because the real world is not an ideal setting (it doesn't set itself out for researchers) probability sampling often proves not feasible. Below are the main problems:

1. A list (sampling frame) may not exist or be possible (for example, shoppers in a particular store, parents of high-level autistic children).
2. If a list exists it may not be accessible, for practical or ethical reasons (the data may be 'buried' in institutional records; they may be seen as too confidential). Access to survey subjects is, in any case, an underestimated problem (see Chapter 4).
3. Even if you have a complete list you may not get a cooperative response from the individuals you identify. It is little use claiming the virtues of a probability sample of 200 if half those contacted don't respond. The 100 who do will have an unknown relationship to the population as a whole and may be a very different group from those who don't.

In short, if you can get a probability sample you should do so; if not you should consider the alternatives described in the next chapter. However, before we proceed to that there are variants of random sampling which, to some extent, overcome the difficulties outlined.

Systematic sampling

This variant of random sampling does not use a table of random numbers (except for the first one chosen). So to obtain a 10 per cent sample from our hypothetical school with 2,000 students, we could take every twentieth student but the *first* one would be identified from a table of random numbers, taking the first pair of digits between 01 and 20, in this case the very first number (square brackets). For example:

Table 2.4 Determining the first number in a systematic sample

[17]53 77 58 71 71 41 61 50 72   12 41 94 96 26   44 95 27 36 99   02 96 74 30 83

90 26 59 21 19   23 52 23 33 12   96 93 02 18 39   07 02 18 36 07   25 99 32 70 23

41 23 52 55 99   31 04 49 69 96   10 47 48 45 88   13 41 43 89 20   97 17 14 49 17

60 20 50 81 69   31 99 73 68 68   35 81 33 03 76   24 30 12 48 60   18 99 10 72 34

91 25 38 05 90   94 58 28 41 36   45 37 59 03 09   90 35 57 29 12   82 62 54 65 60

The numbers in our sampling frame would then be: 17, 37, 57, 77, 97 and so on. A limitation of systematic sampling is that it can be biased by groupings within the list. This may not be important in a school of mixed-ability classes but, where there is doubt, it is advisable to put all the students in strictly alphabetical order first – easily done by computer.

Stratified sampling

An underlying principle of random or systematic sampling is that everyone in the sampling frame has an equal chance of being selected. But this can mean that minority groups within the population scarcely appear at all. If differences between these sub-groups and the majority groupings are the focus of the research, then we need to do something about it.

Say, for example, in a factory workforce of 5,000 the research purpose is to investigate the reasons behind various subgroups (by gender, religious affiliation, ethnic origin or whatever) being unevenly distributed across different employment grades then, to get equivalent numbers across different-sized groupings, you have to sample more frequently across the least-represented groups or *strata* – hence *stratified.*

If you were to take a 5 per cent sample (250 people from 5,000) evenly across the group but only 10 per cent (500) of the *total* group is of ethnic minority origins then there would only be about 25 of them in a random sample. You could decide to take a 50 per cent sample of that group, i.e. 125, and 125 from the main ethnic group (approximately 2.8 per cent of 4,500). Of course there might be more than one subgroup of interest, but the basic procedure is the same. The point is that although the *percentages* within each subgroup are different, the principle of random selection is preserved. The use of a *disproportionate* (rather than a generally pro-rata, proportionate) sampling procedure does not alter its quantitative representativeness.

Multi-stage sampling

This is an extension of what is sometimes known as *cluster* sampling, where you randomly select units or clusters (parliamentary constituencies or wards, job centres, universities and so on) and then, in successive stages, work down to the level of sampling individuals.

Multi-stage sampling can be a big, expensive and extended procedure: but not necessarily so. It is commonly used in political opinion polling where first large geographical areas (however defined) and then parliamentary constituencies are randomly selected: within which a *quota sample* is obtained, usually at high speed, to provide an opinion poll result for a newspaper or broadcasting company that wants rapid, up-to-date and reasonably accurate data on voting intentions and related matters. The use of non-random quota sampling at this last stage is the weak link (quite apart from the fact that it samples *opinions* and *intentions* rather than actual voting behaviour). Bearing that in mind, it is often surprisingly accurate: but see the extended consideration given in the next chapter.

To return to the issue of cost: multi-stage sampling can be a relatively inexpensive way of getting the bigger picture. If, for example, you were interested in the reasons for undergraduates studying civil engineering, focusing on the probable gender imbalance, a simple two-stage procedure could be adopted.

Stage One: Taking a random sample – say, 25 per cent – of English universities offering civil engineering courses.

Stage Two: Taking a random sample (stratified if necessary) of 10 per cent of the students on these courses.

If you then end up with 200 students to be sent a questionnaire you might also decide to carry out in-depth interviews with a sub-group, however composed and selected (e.g. female students). In total this is feasible for a lone researcher but could yield data with a reasonable claim to *empirical generalization,* i.e. data which could be regarded as reflecting the bigger picture.

3

Non-probability Sampling Methods

It has to be said that these methods are more likely to be used in small-scale surveys: the main reason being their greater practicality, not least that often they are the only methods possible. Let us deal with the least respectable first.

Convenience sampling

None of the published authorities has a good word to say about this 'first come, first served' approach to sampling. Robson in his excellent book *Real World Research* (first edition 1993) writes: 'Convenience sampling is sometimes used as a cheap and dirty way of doing a sample survey. It does not produce representative findings' (p. 141). He does go on to say 'There are sensible uses of convenience sampling, but they are more to do with getting a feel for the issues involved, or piloting a proper sample' (p. 141). These last points are not unimportant ones and do indicate how convenience sampling may prove useful.

It is an obvious nonsense to include in a convenience sample people who are quite unlike those in the population of interest. A sample which comprises mainly male academics is unlikely to have anything valid to say about the experience of largely female call-centre staff: an extreme example but given to emphasize the point.

In assembling a convenience sample the key question for the researcher is: are the people in this sample similar to those in the target group? If so they can be useful in several ways:

1. They will enable you to get a sense of the issues (perhaps in the context of a *focus group* – see p. 34–5).
2. You can derive topics or questions for your survey instruments (interviews or questionnaires) better than just working out of the top of your head. Whatever the limitations of the procedure it beats armchair speculation by a mile – with data from the real world to challenge the researcher.
3. You can get some indication of the likely trends in a better organized study. In other words, your mind will be moving in the direction your research might have to take.
4. Finally, and the most contentious assertion of all, such a sample might be more generalizable than is supposed. Because error is unknown it does not mean that generalization is entirely unwarranted. If you've ever listened to poll declarations on election night you will know that very soon the psephologists are saying: *if* these results are indicative of a general trend then X or Y party will be returned with a majority of so many seats. These are 'convenience' samples where general characteristics cannot validly be claimed: yet they exhibit a trend which assumes its own impetus. A small 'reality' sample is likely to be a better index than none at all or any amount of speculation before the event.

This last point is certainly a debatable one but is intended to counter the blanket condemnation that convenience sampling normally receives. Carefully considered, it is a technique with its uses even if it does not meet certain psychometric criteria. The next technique described is little more than a well-focused variant of this.

Purposive sampling

The term 'purposive sampling' is used when researchers have a clear idea of the kind of group they are interested in and an approximate idea of what they want to find out – and sample accordingly. For example, junior hospital doctors' experience of their work during the first 3 years post-qualification; or women who give birth to their first baby after the age of 40. The use of surveys here is often a preliminary to a more focused in-depth qualitative investigation.

Studies of this character are often carried out within the conceptual framework of *grounded theory* (Glaser and Strauss 1967) where the interest is in emerging explanations which account for the data progressively uncovered and where the researcher is asking: how do I understand or explain what I am finding? This emergent process is linked to the notion of *theoretical sampling* – the extent or range of theories (explanations) progressively developed; which reaches a point where the range cannot be further extended – the notion of *theoretical saturation*. This is the kind of abstract textbook paragraph where your eye glides over the words and you wonder what they mean in practice. Let us stay with it for a moment before bringing it down to earth because there is another point to be made.

Research of this kind typically comprises a series of *case studies* for which empirical generalization cannot be claimed, but where the contribution to knowledge is more likely to be in the form of *theoretical generalization* – that the explanations developed may be applied to other individuals or groups even though their characteristics may be different. For example, the explanation of the effects of motherhood on a group of professionally qualified women (e.g. lawyers) in terms of their attitude to work, may also serve to explain parallel experiences of women at quite different levels of education and in different occupational categories. The generation of theory is in any case one of the main purposes of research whatever the methodological stance.

Snowball sampling

The term almost explains itself: you pick up the numbers in your sample as you go along. The researcher knows what category of individual they are after but no list, as such, exists. I used this process myself when looking for mothers who had had a Down's syndrome baby as their first child and were staying at home to look after them. I wanted the mothers to keep records of their child's first 50 words (a difficult thing to do if you are coping with another child as well). Because the parents of Down's syndrome children are part of a network, having identified two such families with the aid of the local branch of the Down's syndrome Association, I was able to make contact with others who knew others and so on. Although a small longitudinal study these were scarce data (comparing Down's syndrome children's vocabulary content and growth pattern with that of 'normal' children) and, despite its imperfections, the study led to some discoveries that I still feel were important.

So 'snowball sampling' is just a way of identifying hard-to-find members of a distinctly defined group. As in my case, your initial point of contact will be the first link in a chain of connections.

Quota sampling

If convenience sampling is typically treated as beyond the pale in research methods texts, quota sampling is usually referred to as if it were not entirely academically respectable. For example, Bryman (2001): '[it is] comparatively rarely employed in academic social research, but is used intensively in commercial research, such as market research and political opinion polling' (p. 99). The implication is that the method is not for the scrupulous.

The kind of commercial research Bryman refers to seeks to construct a 'representative' sample in terms of those demographic characteristics typical of large-scale, complete or probability-sample surveys like the National Census, the *General Household Survey* and so on. Among other things these provide information on the proportions of the population in terms of occupational class, income, area of residence, ethnic origin and age level. Taking these proportional strata, the on-the-ground researchers are given a quota for the various categories usually in multiple format (so many white lower-middle-class males in the age range 45–54 and so on).

As you walk through a crowded shopping centre you can see the opinion pollsters/market researchers scanning passers-by looking for suitable victims. It requires no great sophistication to see that the researchers pick likely candidates in terms of category descriptors but also because they look possibly willing: an interesting source of bias.

To use a cliché of the moment, this is hardly 'rocket science'. And yet . . . certainly, the main weakness is the untestable claim to quantitative representativeness. Equally certainly a *complete* probability sample on the same scale would be entirely superior *if it could be achieved*. But it rarely can, for two reasons, previously cited, but which warrant repetition:

- a complete list to sample from is often not available or difficult to access;
- more importantly, there is usually a high refusal or non-response rate which completely destroys the probability sample's claim to representativeness.

In the latter case a pro-rata quota sample is more representative. Textbook perfection is fine for textbooks but in a real-world research context such abstract principles may carry little weight. With a 30 per cent response rate in a probability sample – a typical response to questionnaires – you will have little information on the different characteristics of the response and non-response group (mainly the latter).

Quota representativeness

The kind of main population-level parameters outlined above are not likely to be relevant to small-scale investigations. But there are more specialized populations with their own parameters such as dental surgeons in an area health authority or undergraduates in a university faculty. The dentists will be in different kinds of practice (private/NHS/both, single-handed/multiple); undergraduates in different departments and at different stages of their course.

A pro-rata quota sample will provide a fair approximation to the character of the total 'population'. The quota can be structured according to those variables that most simply make up the group: these are largely self-evident (as above). But these variables can also be determined by the *purpose* of the research. This is one of the strengths of quota sampling and, in fact, points to its main uses. *Research is about getting answers to research questions –* and this means that data-collection techniques have to be structured so as to give relevant answers.

Other uses of quota sampling

Typically in small-scale investigations the quotas serve the purpose of ensuring that there are enough respondents in different categories along particular variables (note once again that a 'variable' is simply an attribute in which people differ or 'vary').

To translate these abstract terms into a practical example: I had an undergraduate student who was interested in attitudes to the physical punishment of children in Glasgow. She was interested in how people differed in terms of their approval/qualified approval/disapproval of hitting children. That was one variable. The other variables were of the subject descriptor variety: gender, social class, income level, age level. These could be further subdivided depending on what the data would stand, i.e. with sufficient numbers in each category for significant differences to be apparent, if they existed.

23

She used a recording schedule (see Chapter 9) which took no more than 10 minutes to administer. It was mainly composed of 'closed' questions where the answer is indicated (agree/disagree, etc.) but there were a couple of open-ended questions where she was trawling for views that were not quite so straightforward. She stood outside Marks and Spencer in Glasgow's Argyle Street and in ten days collected a little over 200 respondents.

The main focus of interest was whether there were statistically significant differences in attitudes to physical punishment, according to other variables such as age or gender. Using the test known as *chi square* (see p. 83–4) she did in fact find that *age level* produced the biggest differences.

This kind of approach can be used in conjunction with qualitative methods: for example, exploring attitudes to 'hi-tech' consumer goods. Quite apart from the insights that can be obtained, the *quantitative* (statistical significance) dimension enables the researcher to qualify or expand the qualitative data obtained. However, such statistical significance does depend on collecting a large enough sample. With small numbers such differences may not reach required significance levels (see further discussion in Chapter 13).

4

Gaining Access to the Relevant Group

Access to the group you want to research may not be simple. It is an issue often neglected by textbooks (though Robson 1993, pp. 294–302 is a notable exception). The problems are partly practical, partly ethical. Ethical issues apart, the world is not a ready-made series of lists with identified points of contact for the researcher.

Assuming that you know, broadly, the kind of group you're interested in (veterinary surgeons, users of complementary medicine, men who have been made redundant after the age of 50), how do you know where to find them?

It is like breaking into a circle: you need to find a point of entry. In practice, personal contacts are the best way in. A networking process is involved: a friend knows someone who works in a riding stable and is married to a vet; someone else knows the owner of a shop selling 'health' products; a neighbour who works in a job centre knows of an agency which specializes in relocating those made redundant in mid-career. These 'specialized informants' can short-cut the process and also introduce a note of realism into over-optimistic research plans: vets are bombarded with junk mail and routinely bin it; purveyors of health products may have a protective attitude towards their customers; ethical criteria loom large when issues as sensitive as redundancy are involved. Real-world research is beset by such practicalities.

Getting a list

A list (sampling frame) may not exist as such and, even if it does, access to it may be difficult or prohibited. If a list is unobtainable then some variant of snowball sampling is the main option, provided that you are fairly clear about your research purpose and the kind of people you are looking for.

Of course, you don't need a list if the group is large and can easily be encountered in the street, or by telephone (see Chapter 10). Defined groups, such as police officers, are another matter because even if you can get a list of names you may find barriers to access.

Quite simply, over the past 10 to 20 years information about personal details has become not just a more sensitive issue but an ethical one, enshrined in formal legislation and related regulations. This is in addition, but related, to the ethical procedures insisted on by universities, the professions and government institutions. You will often not get a list without formal permission as to its use, after scrutiny of the purposes and procedures of the research.

Since surveys are not normally particularly intrusive in their content and are not best suited to matters of sensitivity, the ethical dimension may not be of prime importance. But awareness of its implications for research practice needs to be considered. Chapter 2 of *Research Interviewing: The Range of Techniques* (Gillham 2005) provides a review of the topic at the practical level of what to do about it. The main ethical requirements for surveys are that you should make the *purpose* of your research clear to those involved and obtain their consent to use the information they disclose, protecting confidentiality as appropriate.

Defining your purpose

Published papers give the impression that researchers know exactly where they are going from the start, but this is *post hoc* reconstructed logic. The reality of the research process does not have that neat line of logic and there is a powerful argument for writing up research 'as it happens' – a more truthful account and more helpful to the novice. Research purposes and questions develop as you engage in the empirical activity of seeking answers. You need some prior familiarity with the relevant literature (but what's 'relevant' becomes clearer as you progress). It is also helpful to talk to other researchers in the area of interest. Like many other specialisms, research is not something you just learn from books.

But the main clarifier is tentative engagement with people in the roughly defined group of interest: empirical reality focuses both content and methods. This is why, in later chapters, emphasis is placed on the importance of trialling questions and topics in developing even the restricted coverage of a short questionnaire or interview schedule. To yield data of reasonable quality the focus of your research tool needs to be clear and *tested*: desk work is not enough.

Patience is required because the process of preparation and defining your objectives go hand-in-hand. When you have clarified your purpose, and refined your data-collection techniques, only then do you have a chance of doing a half-decent project.

Negotiating access to organizations

Organizations are something of a special case and represent a distinct challenge as far as access is concerned but they offer a number of advantages in carrying out a survey. Boundaries are clear and so is the framework for sampling. Members can be identified and located within a structured hierarchy while lines of formal communication are usually well-established.

The initial stage is finding out where you can get first-hand information about the organization. This is where networking comes in: a teacher in a school, a sales assistant in a large retail company, a nurse in a hospital, a production manager in a factory. The value of these contacts is that they can give you insight into the *informal* reality and the culture or ethos of the organization. The formal dimension can be picked up, usually, from an institutional website, PR publications and the like.

From the same sources you can also find out whom to approach (and how) for formal permission which probably entails a written application. For this you will need to prepare a project outline (not more than one side of A4 at the most – senior managers are addicted to crisply written bullet points).

An organization is not necessarily a physical entity: a profession is an organization but widely scattered and made up of individuals and small groups (a similarly diverse connotation applies to the concept of a *case* – often thought of as only applying to an individual). But however the organization is made up there is a need to give thought to its characteristics at a formal level of study. Recommended for this purpose is *Doing Research in Organizations* (1988) edited by the ethnographer, Alan Bryman. Of particular interest is the chapter by Buchanan, Boddy and McCalman engagingly titled 'Getting in, getting on, getting out and getting back': the point being that there is much more to doing research in social contexts than obtaining permission to do so. In any case this permission may be little more than allowing you to approach other people, i.e. *levels* of permission.

The basic procedure

The important thing is to demonstrate that you are well-organized.

1. Be as clear as you can about what you are trying to do (but emphasize that you need guidance and advice).

2. Communicate this as widely as you can: people like to feel informed. ('This is the first I've heard about it' presages trouble.)
3. Make sure you consult all relevant parties. (I know of a questionnaire survey that was blocked because no one had thought to consult the relevant trade union whose members were being surveyed.)
4. Have a detailed schedule that nonetheless leaves room for flexibility.
5. Carry out initial consultations, e.g. on the content and wording of a questionnaire: not only useful (making for a better questionnaire) but also allowing participants to have a degree of ownership.
6. Be efficient, economical of other people's time and, above all, keep your promises.
7. Communicate findings – perhaps in a very summary report in a newsletter, on a website or via a small slot in a staff meeting.
8. When you leave make your indebtedness clear, both verbally and in a more formal written note; and leave the door ajar (getting back) as there may be things you want to follow up (interviews to back up survey data, future research). Handled in the right way, this may be a useful seam to exploit.

5

Focusing Survey Topics and Questions

The popularity of questionnaires is probably because it's assumed they are easy to construct, and that they constitute a rapid means of obtaining a sackful of data. Such carelessly assembled data-sets are worthless as research even though they figure often enough in the media.

The easier it is to get research data the less likely it is that they will be worthwhile. Students are often hypnotized by quantity: the magic of numbers. But 500 badly constructed postal questionnaires are vastly inferior to 20 well-constructed face-to-face interviews. More than that even a well-constructed questionnaire will not be a match in depth and subtlety of detail for a skilfully conducted interview. Of course the data are of different kinds: questionnaire data are primarily quantitative (you count and classify the responses), interview data primarily qualitative (you categorize and interpret the responses).

Survey data are inherently superficial as you don't know what lies behind the responses, and no amount of statistical manipulation will tell you. They also offer little scope for discovery, for the unexpected, because the range of answers is largely predetermined and presented in a choice format (*agree/ disagree/ not sure* and so on). Their best use is to provide a descriptive framework and to identify areas or topics where further in-depth research is required. Like a series of trial drillings they can indicate where a more extensive exploration phase might be worthwhile. This descriptive and guiding function needs to be well-based; for a survey instrument to be useful you have to be sure that it taps into areas of interest (in oil test-drilling terms the equivalent of a geological survey).

Exploring the topic area

Some 20 years ago I was commissioned by the then Committee of Principals and Vice-Chancellors to carry out a survey of university technicians' 'job satisfaction'. This was part of a big job-restructuring exercise and had full union support. Having worked in universities for a long time, at one level I knew many technical staff quite well but not at the level of comprehensive detail of their experience of their jobs. Since the upshot of my commission would be a postal questionnaire, the results of which would be contributory to major changes in pay and career structure for technicians, it was obviously necessary to get it right. In other words it was vital to make sure that what went into the questionnaire tapped into those issues which were important for the respondents (and where their responses would inform their employers).

Working with colleagues in a random sample of UK universities, and taking a quota sample of different grades within them, we carried out open interviews with this sample, essentially asking: 'What sort of things do you like about your job and what are your dissatisfactions and frustrations?'

These comparatively short (30-minute) interviews were tape-recorded. We didn't transcribe them in full but listened, in a play-through, for *substantive* statements: those points of importance which could contribute to question focus and construction. In practice it was quite easy to identify likely topics.

I then had the task of doing a *categorical analysis* of these substantive statements, i.e. grouping statements of similar content together. There was a surprising degree of commonality: some issues were clearly of prime concern. One interesting point was that not only did we derive key question topics from this exercise but often *forms of words* as well. The way the technicians expressed *their* meaning was often better than anything we could have come up with. The result was a questionnaire with a more authentic 'voice'.

And this is the main lesson: *that you should allow the survey group (or a sample from it) to tell you what issues are important.* In this way you avoid doing irrelevant research and get a more valid response (the questions touch on something that the respondents can recognize or appreciate) and also a *better response rate* (more questionnaires returned).

Data quality and response rate are a direct consequence of the preparation phase: we'll now consider this more generally in practical terms.

Where do you start?

Students seem to fall into two groups: those who want to get on with 'doing their research' having read very little on their topic; and those who read widely because they don't want to start their empirical research until they are 'ready'.

In fact, reading round the topic and making the first tentative steps along the empirical path need to go together, each informing the other in an iterative progression. Past a certain point there is something a bit deadening about undiluted desk work. It is rightly called *secondary* research: the recycling of what other researchers have done and what they thought about the topic. The freshness of your own first-hand data (*primary* research) is a tonic from the real world, even when the data are of a very preliminary and patchy quality. Almost immediately what you are finding will start to qualify what you have read and point to further focused reading.

The essential preliminaries

1. Identify your area of interest: by this is meant putting it down on paper with your justification. Writing down your early thoughts/intentions is part of the clarification process.
2. Search for key books and research journal papers – particularly the latter because they're more up to date and report original research. This can be a time-consuming process even in these days of computerized databases. You will normally need access to a university library system linked to expensive subscription databases: don't assume you'll find worthwhile papers free on the Web. Out there somewhere is a key paper which will speak to your topic directly. And don't expect to find it right away; to some extent you only come to know what you're looking for by getting on with your empirical investigation.
3. Identify someone who is an expert in your area or experienced in the style of research you are engaged in. In university terms a suitable supervisor is a lifeline. They can head you off from unprofitable directions, guide your reading but, above all, encourage *you* to clarify what you are about, both verbally in a supervision session and by writing summary reports and drafts.
4. Make a start by exploring topics in discussion with members of your intended survey population. *You begin in this way with whatever instrument you plan to use in the survey itself* (face-to-face interview, questionnaire, telephone interview).
5. And finally, if you are a member of the group you plan to survey do not fall into the trap of assuming that you already know the topics of relevance and what questions need asking. It isn't just a case of one's own experience or viewpoint not being typical. *It is that we don't know the group as a researcher.* More than that we don't know *ourselves* in that way: which is why, when interviewed, we can find ourselves coming up with material that we scarcely realized we had to offer. Our relationship with colleagues or acquaintances is not (thankfully) that of a researcher. And when we approach them from

that perspective we come to see them (ourselves?) differently. The social research stance is always to approach our own area as though it were unknown territory. Which it is.

Narrowing the focus

Interviews are of different kinds and for different purposes (selection, for example) but here we are talking about research interviews. The main dimension of difference is in the degree of structure. When you know precisely what it is you want to find out you can use a (time-economical) *structured interview*. When you only know the broad area of interest and cannot anticipate even the main topics, you use a more-or-less *unstructured interview*, which you employ to get preliminary guidance from your survey group. The approach to take is that you are planning a survey and need guidance as to what you should cover.

You start very simply. If, for example, your area of interest is the kind of support provided for parents of autistic children you might begin by talking to just one parent. Even one such interview can cause a rapid readjustment of your assumptions. Your next (and any subsequent) interviews will find you progressively better prepared as the main themes or topics become apparent: key issues that need further exploration, as well as side issues that are harder to evaluate.

Seeing people individually not only gives a detailed intensive picture but has a particular kind of personal dynamic and one that both guides and motivates you as a researcher. Using *focus groups* is a further stage in topic development once you are clearer as to your direction. A focus group is a similarly open approach but you need to come to it with an outline plan of the areas to be covered. Otherwise you can find yourself in a rather chaotic situation: you need to know enough to steer or *focus* the discussion.

Such a group is focused in two ways:

- in terms of the *group membership* – chosen so as to be directly relevant to the topic area;
- in terms of the *topic* – so that you and the group know what is to be discussed.

The group should be neither too small nor too large – big enough for a dynamic to emerge, not so many that some members don't get a look in. Part of the 'management' of the group is ensuring that everyone has their say. An ideal number is around eight. Fewer than six is too few; more than ten too many. In practice it is a good idea to have *two* researchers at a focus group – one to manage or 'facilitate', the other to record key or novel elements that are thrown up by the rapid movement of the debate, which can get quite lively. It is often interesting to observe how differently people you have interviewed individually behave in this setting.

Areas of disagreement can be key elements for the research (a range of views and experience, unresolved questions); but, even with those topics you are aware of, the degree of feeling about them that can emerge in a focus group is illuminating in itself. There is something to be pursued here (further reading, a shift in topics and questions).

Preliminary reading and preliminary research create their own momentum: you move back and forth from one to the other. Your reading throws up things that you ask about. What members of your survey group have to say qualifies what you've read – or sends you back to the library or computer to fill a gap in your formal knowledge or to rethink your approach. This is the creative stage of research: it is both exhausting and, if you are lucky, compelling.

6

The Relationship between Questions and Answers

Forming specific questions, the fine grain of survey research, is not the start of such a project but about half-way along the development phase. More than that: like the writer of a murder mystery who sets out the plot knowing how it is to be resolved, so in writing questions you need to be clear *in what way* they are to be answered.

Open and closed questions

The issue of what questions you want to ask and how you want to ask them comes down to *how the responses are to be analysed*. To recap, there are basically two kinds of questions: those where the answer is left 'open' and those where the answer is 'closed' – in the sense of offering a limited range of specified answers. An open question might be:

- Which daily newspaper do you read most often?

A closed equivalent might be:

- Which of the following daily newspapers do you read most often? (Followed by a list with tick boxes and probably an 'other' category.)

The closed version, with its simple tick response, is a more efficient way of posing the question and less trouble to answer. It also prompts people, reminding them of elements they might overlook. With specific 'factual' questions about *behaviour* (what people *do*) there is not much of a problem: the closed question works well.

However, when you are dealing with *opinions* the choice is not so clear-cut. For example, if you wanted to survey attitudes to the war in Iraq an open question could be:

• What were your views, at the time, on the Allied invasion of Iraq in 2003?

That is a complicated question which, as it is posed, may require a complicated and extended answer. If you have 100 – or a 1,000 – such answers in a postal questionnaire you have an enormous task of analysing (or categorizing) the responses. And if they are part of a questionnaire similarly constructed then it becomes an almost impossible task particularly for a lone researcher. Indeed, much simpler (and less emotive) questions than this will pose problems of analysis. It is not that the question is not worth asking but that it is inappropriate to the medium of a postal question-naire; there being other reasons such as the need to *explore* the answers given. This is where in-depth face-to-face interviews would be more appropriate.

A *closed* version of the above question might be:

SAME QUESTION (Please tick the most appropriate box below):

☐ Broadly in favour
☐ Not sure/no opinion
☐ Mainly against

Note that it is the *answer* that is closed, not the question. This is called a *pre-coded* format. It is then a simple matter to analyse the answers – a basic count formula. The weakness of such a pre-coded analysis is that it doesn't tell you much: but to expect it to

37

do so is to misunderstand not just the practicalities of forming questions for a questionnaire but also what you can expect of such a survey. Questionnaire (or other) survey instruments are best at:

- providing a straightforward 'descriptive' account of the wider framework;
- indicating those areas where further in-depth research is necessary (perhaps where the balance of responses is unexpected or shows up subgroup differences).

Constructing survey questions

In constructing a questionnaire you may find that the range of possible answers alters the way in which you frame the question. This is because the answers almost always follow some kind of multiple-choice format. There are not so many of these, but using a variety is a way of keeping your respondent interested. Here are some examples where we give the *answers* first, for emphasis:

- YES/NO Have you seen your doctor during the past year?

• up to 1 week		If YES how long did you have to wait for an appointment? (TICK ONE BOX)
• 1 – 2 weeks		
• 2 – 3 weeks		*NB This choice of direction linked to a previous*
• more than 3 weeks		*question is called routing a response.*

• very satisfied		How satisfied were you with the consultation? (TICK ONE BOX)
• satisfied		
• not satisfied		
• very dissatisfied		

This last kind of scale, widely used and often with more choice (5 to 7 options) including a neutral one in the centre ('not sure' or similar) tends to produce a positive *response bias* – perhaps the reason why it is so popular with commercial enterprises! To get negative responses, or simply the full range of answers, you often have to resort to a *forced choice*. For example:

● time allocated	In the consultation with your doctor, what was the **most** satisfactory part (TICK √) and what was the **least** satisfactory (CROSS X)?
● feeling that you were listened to	
● diagnostic advice	
● explanation of treatment	
● follow-up appointments	

Another way to get people to express a preferential judgement is to *weight* a set of scaled responses so as to emphasize that you are interested in critical judgements set against a *positive* statement ('Well, I don't agree with *that.*') For instance:

● The Health Centre provides a very good appointments service (TICK ONE BOX).
□ agree
□ not sure
□ disagree
□ strongly disagree

An alternative is to put different elements in rank order, as a way of expressing judgements. For example, if the Health Centre runs a weight-control programme, you might ask the following:

● Which aspect of the programme did you find most useful? Put 1 against what you found **most** useful, 2 against the next most useful, and so on down to 5 for the **least** useful.
□ scientific information
□ fallacies about dieting
□ advice on healthy eating
□ information on unhealthy eating (what to avoid)
□ changing exercise patterns

The strength of this technique is that it gives the researcher a better idea of the relative merits of the different components of the programme. Note that because numbers are used it is tempting to construct an average 'score' and this is not legitimate (see p. 90–1).

Specified response questions

Where possible you should provide the probable answers so that the respondent simply has to check a given choice. But sometimes you know what *kind* of answer you want but the range of *exact* responses cannot be identified or there would be too many to list. For example:

- Where did you do your teacher training?
  Please write in: _____

- In what year did you complete your training?
  Please write in: _____

- In what year did you obtain your first teaching post?
  Please write in: _____

Here the required responses are more simply obtained, and can then be classified as appropriate.

Slightly open questions

The trouble with questionnaire judgements of the multiple-choice variety is that you don't know *why* a particular answer was chosen. If your aim is to improve the quality of service it is here that adverse judgements need amplification. If, for example, in relation to the Health Centre appointments service some respondents have ticked either *strongly disagree* or *disagree*, then in order to take action you need to know what lies behind the judgement. To get more insight you can phrase what is known as an *indicated response* where you are indicating the required answer but not saying what it should be:

- If you have ticked either **disagree** or **strongly dis-agree**, please say why:

_____

_____

The responses to this will require a simple content-analysis approach (see Chapter 14). But do not be deceived by that word 'simple': categorizing open responses is a time-consuming business. Questions of this type should be of the essential variety and few in number – probably no more than two. Problems of analysis apart, they are more trouble to answer and may impair your response rate. If there is one index of those who lack experience in constructing questionnaires it is that they include a lot of loosely constructed open questions.

Subject descriptor questions

This category has been left till last because it is the most straightforward yet often the most carelessly constructed for that reason.

The answers to subject descriptor questions are important because they allow you to carve up the questions and answers that follow (the focus of the survey research) in terms of differences on the subject descriptors (gender, age, income, occupational status, educational level, marital status). Their very 'factuality' may suggest that there is no problem in getting this information. But there are two issues: that the questions should be entirely unambiguous; and that they should be sensitive to people's feelings about the information that is sought.

Gender may be an easy one. But asking people about their _age_ is another matter. Consider the following which shows a common error:

- Please tick the box against your age range:

□ 20–30
□ 30–40
□ 40–50
□ 50–60
□ 60–70
□ 70 +

So which box do you tick if you are 30 or 40 or 50, etc.? The format needs to be:

□ 20–29
□ 30–39
– and so on.

The 10-year range is adequate for most purposes; a 5-year range is a possible alternative if it is really necessary. People are remarkably vain about their age presumably because they like to think they don't look it. So you don't ask for an exact age, except perhaps in the case of the under-20s.

Income is another sensitive area. Depending upon your survey group you may opt for £10,000 or £5,000 intervals. Here a single-digit overlap in the categories is unimportant because people don't know their income precisely. So:

- Please tick the box against your gross annual income range:

□ under £10,000
□ £10,000–20,000
□ £20,000–30,000
□ £30,000–40,000
□ £40,000–50,000
□ £50,000 +

The ceiling income indicated, as well as the size of the steps, should take into account the probable range in the group being surveyed. The above example would be too high and too coarsely graded for undergraduate students, or pensioners for example.

Occupational status is, again, not entirely straightforward. In the standardized world we inhabit, financial institutions are thrown by those who do not fit the single categories: *employed, retired, unemployed* or *self-employed*. So we might offer the following choice:

□ Full-time employed
□ Part-time employed
□ Unemployed
□ Retired
□ Self-employed
□ Unwaged carer (of children or adults)

You are usually asked to tick one box. But in my case, for example, I am both retired (no 'job') and self-employed (writer, consultant) and until last year I was also part-time employed. So which box should I tick? An appropriate instruction might be: *Tick all relevant boxes.*

Occupational category is commonly used as an index of social class or socio-economic status but that is not without its critics – *educational level* is another (but correlated) dimension – see below. You can't expect people to classify themselves socially and there is much disagreement among social scientists; for those interested, look at the debates in *Twentieth Century British Social Trends* edited by A. H. Halsey and Josephine Webb (2000).

Classifications by occupation are traditionally divided between manual and non-manual and further sub-divided (professional, semi-professional, routine white-collar workers, small-business workers, skilled manual, semi-skilled and unskilled). At one time these correlated quite closely with income and educational level but that is no longer the case particularly in relation to income; many 'manual' workers are now educationally well qualified while many 'white-collar' workers are not. In any case the subjective perceptions of social class are subtler than such 'objective' descriptive categories: social behaviour, accent, clothes, styles of grooming, tastes and habits of mind loom large here.

Although occupational category is one variable of importance, in small-scale surveys you are not usually seeking to mimic main population-level parameters. For guidance on classifying occupations in the UK the reader is referred to the *General Household Survey* (ONS 2006). So, however you use the information you can ask:

- What is your current job (or your last job if caring for others, unemployed or retired)? _____

Educational level is a less ambiguous way of classifying people than their occupation with its bewildering diversity. In the UK you could specify it as follows:

- Please tick the **highest** level of your educational qualifications:
☐ None
☐ GCSE (Grades D to G)
☐ GCSE (Grade C or above)
☐ A level or equivalent (e.g. Scottish Highers, NVQ Level 3)
☐ First degree or graduate level professional qualification
☐ Postgraduate qualification (diploma or certificate)
☐ Master's degree
☐ Doctorate

Marital status is, if anything, even trickier. The once standard choice: Married/Divorced/Separated/Single no longer applies. Many people co-habit (and the partnership may not be heterosexual). How do you classify that? And we now have the category of 'civil partnership' between same sex couples.

A more adequate choice would be:

☐ married
☐ separated
☐ divorced

☐ widowed
☐ single
☐ civil partnership
☐ in a stable relationship

As with the occupational category, people should be given the choice of ticking more than one box, e.g. 'divorced' and 'in a stable relationship', if they so wish.

In the next chapter we deal with question development. The present chapter (in illogical order) means that when you come to draft a possible question you will at the same time be thinking: How shall I set out the answer choices? Which answer format would work best?

This process is part of what is involved in producing clear and well-focused questions. And that stage is fundamental to producing a questionnaire or structured interview that works: one that the respondent can interpret unambiguously and where the researcher gets the kind of information that is being sought.

7

Refining the Questions

The last chapter emphasized the need to consider how questions might be answered because this has a bearing on how they are framed. But questions might be presented slightly differently according to the data-collection method used:

- a printed *questionnaire*, which respondents have to complete by themselves;
- a structured face-to-face interview (essentially a personally administered questionnaire, which we refer to as a *recording schedule*);
- a structured *telephone interview*, which falls somewhere between the two in that we suggest you send the respondents a questionnaire and talk them through it.

But whichever method you choose, the process of question development is the same; it is only later that certain adjustments might be made depending on how the questions are to be presented.

The unstructured phase

How much time you devote to this stage depends on the degree of familiarity with the topic area. The mistake is to think you know it so well that this open 'finding out' procedure can be bypassed altogether.

46

It involves talking to people who are members of (or similar to) the potential survey group. As indicated in Chapter 5 this can be done systematically with short unstructured interviews that you tape-record and content-analyse, in a focus group (a slightly later stage where you're fairly clear what you want to focus on), or by informal conversations, which may be all that is feasible.

Where possible audio-recording should be used, as written note-taking interrupts the flow, distracts your attention and involves on-the-hoof selection that may be ill-judged. And if you just rely on recollected impressions you will lose a lot of material. There is much to be said for listening carefully to a tape-recorded conversation (perhaps more than once) where attention is focused on the *content* and not on maintaining the interaction. Writing down the substantive topics that come up also clarifies your thinking, even if you are not conscious of the process. In each case you make it clear to the people involved what your area of interest is, that you need guidance on the detail and will be using what they tell you to develop questions for a questionnaire or similar. What are the things *they* think are important?

Brainstorming

You can do this sooner or later: usually when you feel the need to put possible questions down on paper.

This is not the point to concern yourself with exact forms of words, whether the questions fall into groups, are in the wrong order, are different ways of saying the same thing (useful in itself) or – as will certainly be the case – are too many.

You will find that after you've disgorged all this material you will add to it gradually, rather like a shopping list. At this stage don't try to categorize or edit – at least on paper – although that process will be going on in your mind because you can't help it. This element of unconscious work is highly productive and you need to allow time for it to bear fruit.

And for the moment keep the list to yourself while you pick other people's brains.

The Delphi technique

This technique (with its classical reference) can be used in various ways: we use it here as a way of getting further items for your questionnaire/interview. For example, if your research area is people's attitudes to alternative medicine, you ask those with some knowledge of the area for suggested questions (perhaps no more than three or four) that could be included in the questionnaire. You don't show them or tell them what you've drafted so that their ideas are not 'contaminated' by yours.

There is usually some overlap with what you already have but perhaps expressed in a better form of words and, quite often, something is suggested that had not occurred to you.

Sorting questions under topic headings

Logically 'topics' – the groupings of a set of questions – come before the specific questions themselves. For some, whose mental processes are highly organized, that may be the case, but for most of us questions come first – rather out of order – and, by inspection, we can then see how they fall into groups or topics. When we do that, gaps (questions we need to ask) and redundancies (two or more questions that say essentially the same thing) will soon become apparent.

For example, in the fictional instance of a study of alternative medicine we might infer a grouping of questions under the topic heading *Doubts about alternative medicine*, which could be set out as below (with answer formats). (Note how the answer choices are designed to fit the questions or statements.)

a. How do you feel about 'self-prescription'?
   ☐ No problem
   ☐ Not sure
   ☐ Doubtful

b. The advertising is too 'commercial'.
   - ☐ Agree
   - ☐ Not sure
   - ☐ Disagree
c. Do you feel able to choose the right 'medicine'?
   - ☐ Yes
   - ☐ Not always
   - ☐ No
d. Do you feel you understand what is said about using the medicines?
   - ☐ Yes
   - ☐ Not always
   - ☐ Sometimes
e. Are you confident about taking the right amount of medicine?
   - ☐ Yes
   - ☐ Not always
   - ☐ No
f. The advertising tries to 'blind you with science'.
   - ☐ Agree
   - ☐ Not sure
   - ☐ Disagree
g. Are you confident about making the right *choice* of medicine?
   - ☐ Yes
   - ☐ Not always
   - ☐ No

When you read through these you might feel that (a), (c) and (g) are essentially the same; as are (b) and (f); and then possibly (d) and (f); in addition (e) could be seen as overlapping with (a). So the exercise has set you thinking, but you may decide to stay with them all for the moment. The revision process will be helped if you set out similar questions in parallel, i.e. side-by-side rather than having to dot around in a vertically arranged list. You can do this in spreadsheet format on a computer using *Microsoft Excel* or similar; or hand-write them on to blank A3 sheets following a similar format. It is curious how this simple visual rearrangement assists your thinking.

For example:

The advertising is too 'commercial'./ The advertising tries to 'blind you with science'.

Are they equivalent? Is one better than the other?

Writing questions is as much art as science: some people have a definite knack for it. And conversely you can find yourself trapped by the first form of words that occurred to you. You can have doubts about a word or a phrase without being clear as to an alternative. If you highlight these you can come back to them. For example, the phrase 'blinding with science' might seem too strong so that respondents will, inevitably, react against it.

Overlap is one issue, clarity is another, redundancy is yet another. All writing, after the initial formulation, is about revision, particularly eliminating unnecessary words. Repetition and piling on the adjectives (or adverbs) are the main culprits here. For example:

- What was the very first thing that made you decide to give alternative medicine a try?

Please write in: _____

– could be replaced as:

- What made you try alternative medicine?

Please write in: _____

There is no loss of meaning in the revision and its impact is greater. 'Simple' and direct questions always work best because they are better focused, which means the *response* is better focused. Interestingly, in free-flowing face-to-face interviews there is a greater temptation for the interviewer to be more 'wordy', paradoxically when it is harder for the person being interviewed to attend to all that is being asked. A particular tendency is for the interviewer to ask a compound question such as: *Why did you try complementary medicine and what was your health problem at the time?*

That's not one question but two and, in written format, one can see immediately that it won't do. Writing is inherently more economical than speech; although it is worth noting that an expert interview is characterized by the economy of the questions. Perhaps just one word: *Why?*

We need to distinguish *trialling* from *piloting*: these topics are covered in Chapters 8–10. Trialling is where you take your (too long) list of questions – and answer formats – and try them out on a small number of people similar to those in your survey group. You will already have your questions sorted under topic headings with alternatives about which you can't make up your mind. These will be what you present to your trialling group, but one further revision is needed before you do that.

Putting questions in developmental order

Questions in a questionnaire or interview schedule should follow a 'logical' order: where one leads on to the next which, nonetheless, presents something different. If the person being interviewed feels 'I've already answered that question' then the process starts to lose momentum – with an associated irritation factor. One question should also be a kind of orientation or preparation for the next. Hence the emphasis on establishing a logical or developmental sequence. However, the rather piece-meal way that questions are generated means that they won't be in quite that order (if at all). We'll take a practical example.

If you were researching the motivation for, and experience of, 'mature' students (defined as 30+) taking a postgraduate course, you might have a topic heading *Expectations of the course* under which the following questions have been accumulated:

a. Have you found the course as you expected?
   ☐ Yes
   ☐ More or less
   ☐ Not really

b. How accurate did you find the description of the course in the prospectus?
- ☐ Accurate
- ☐ Fairly accurate
- ☐ Inaccurate

c. How have you found the academic level of the course?
- ☐ Higher than expected
- ☐ As expected
- ☐ Lower than expected

d. How have you found the workload on the course?
- ☐ Very heavy
- ☐ About right
- ☐ Easily managed

e. Are your fellow students of the type you had expected?
- ☐ Yes
- ☐ More or less
- ☐ No

f. How well does the course fit what you feel you need?
- ☐ Very well
- ☐ Quite well
- ☐ Not very well

g. Does the course provide the intellectual stimulation you require?
- ☐ Yes
- ☐ Sometimes
- ☐ Not really

How would you revise the order of these questions? Are there any that you feel are essentially the same, or redundant? *Take five minutes to make your own revisions before reading the next paragraph.*

My judgement is that (e) and (f) should come just after (b) – and in reverse order (f) and then (e). Questions (g) and (c) seem pretty well equivalent but it might be worth trying out both to see which works better; (a) is a clear lead in to the questions so should stay first, while (d) could also stay if (f) and (e) were transposed. Your judgement may well differ: all you need to do is review your justification.

8

The Trialling Stage

There are two try-out stages: trialling the *questions* and, after revision, piloting the *questionnaire* (or interview, as the case may be); in both cases you work with people similar to the target group in the main study.

At the moment what you have is something like a much-too-long questionnaire organized, as we've described, under topic headings. We now need to see how these questions (and the answer formats) work, because some of them won't work at all well which can be something of a surprise. If they 'don't work' this will be obvious from the way the individuals you are trying them out with don't *immediately* see what a question means and what they have to do. If they 'misunderstand' or are hesitant then there is something amiss: you either have to make changes, substitute something else or delete the item entirely. In the end what you produce has to work well on its own in a questionnaire, or at speed in a face-to-face or telephone interview.

The procedure is straightforward:

- You have two copies of your overweight questionnaire.
- You give one copy to the person you are working with and have one yourself on which to make notes.
- You explain that you're trying to develop a questionnaire or interview and that you've written a lot of questions – more than you need – and you want to see which ones work best so that you can prune some of them.

● You say that, apart from answering the questions, any other comments or feedback would be useful.

The trialling group

We've emphasized that what you have is a desk-work product – now for the reality test. Working with people similar to your survey group you follow the procedure as above, *reading* the questions so as to pace the respondent. Note that the act of reading out loud in itself may alert you to clumsy constructions and you may find yourself making impromptu changes. You *watch* the respondent, looking for signs of uncertainty or hesitation. You may have to clarify a question (note how you do this) or suggest alternative answer formats (if the choice doesn't fit how they want to respond). When there is a choice of question formats you can ask for their preference.

It is usually quite a shock to find how much revision is pointed up by this simple exercise but on the basis of this you will be producing a draft questionnaire or interview schedule (like the real thing) which you will *pilot*, i.e. use in the way that is intended in the main study.

Whether you plan to use a questionnaire or an interview you adopt the same principle: that ultimately the questions should work without your assistance. Good questions are those that make immediate sense, call forth the sort of response you are seeking and do so without significant hesitation or uncertainty. Those that don't are either candidates for revision or deletion: don't attempt these changes after each individual administration – you need to see whether the difficulties are general. If a question confuses everyone its fate is obvious, though occasional confusions may be less important if you plan to do interviews and can deal with misunderstandings. But if you're planning to use questionnaires and find misunderstandings occur at this stage, even with just one person, that indicates a weakness which may prove more general in the main survey.

You will be making notes on your copy of the 'questionnaire' but it is advisable to tape-record the session as well. Mini-discussions and off-the-cuff comments can be very illuminating and are worth reflecting on later.

Achieving a practicable length

There is one other purpose for this trialling stage: the overall length of time that the questionnaire takes to complete. How long should that be? The answer is in two parts:

- how many people you plan to survey (the more, the shorter the questionnaire in general);
- what the intended respondents' tolerance of the time involved is likely to be (again the shorter the better).

Ten minutes is a tolerable maximum and you can specify this, to reassure your victims: *it won't take more than 10 minutes* (and you'd better be right).

Although in this trialling phase you will be going more slowly, the experience is some kind of guide as to how much pruning will be required. If the trialling session lasts more than 20 minutes the pruning has to be drastic. So what can you cut out? Rewording, deleting questions (redundant or unworkable), modifying answer formats, improving the visual layout (we deal with the principles of questionnaire/interview schedule design in Chapter 9) – all of these things save time as well as fine-tuning the schedule. And, of course, the discursive 'consultation' elements won't apply as they do at the trialling stage. But, like economizing when you find yourself overstretched financially, it might not be enough. To pursue the financial analogy, you may need to restructure your spending, cutting out a major item (like getting rid of your car).

To revert to the schedule, which is organized in sections with several questions in each, it might be necessary to delete a whole topic, or even more than one. This may seem drastic (or a pity) but the issue is one of ending up with a practicable instrument.

Jerome K. Jerome in his classic *Three Men in a Boat* describes the stage of preparation for their journey where they made a list of what would be useful to take with them: it was of a grossly impracticable length. The conclusion was that they were going about it the wrong way: that they shouldn't list the things they could do with, but the things they couldn't do without.

On your schedule some topics will be more important than others: you have to prioritize. And you retain only those topics you can't do without.

Reviewing the content

The first thing is to review what has turned up at the trialling stage. Read through your notes and listen to the recordings. Then with these fresh in your mind (and to be referred to where necessary) you go through an unmarked trialling schedule making the necessary alterations; it is now that you decide on *topic deletions*.

As you word-process the changes you will begin to see the schedule coming into shape as a whole, not just at the level of topics and question wording. And now that content is not the primary concern you can begin to address the issue of the layout. Because how well it works is not simply a matter of getting the words right but whether the design supports the purpose of the schedule, making it attractive and also accessible and easy to follow.

One of the seductive qualities of modern word-processing software is that it is quite easy to produce a questionnaire that 'looks good'. I sometimes suspect this is a factor behind the current rash of questionnaire-based research projects, which don't stand up to scrutiny because their looks are only skin-deep. And the next stage has little to do with these surface qualities.

9

Designing Questionnaires and Interview Schedules

Word-processing question changes is one thing: designing the questionnaire is quite another. You don't try to do this directly on to the computer. An old-fashioned manual cut-and-paste job works best to begin with: cutting out individual questions (under their topic headings) and rearranging them on blank pages. This simple physical activity is an intellectually clarifying one and, even at this point, you will find it necessary to make minor changes to wording so that the sequence dovetails neatly. The 'cut and paste' function on a computer doesn't have quite the same direct feel: however, you may disagree.

1. Don't devote more than half a page to the 'personal descriptor' items at the beginning (you can be economical of space here) and make sure that you only ask for what you are going to use.
2. Briefly explain the purpose of the survey on the front page or, if necessary, on a separate face-sheet in letter form. It may be obvious to you, and you may have communicated it in other ways, but the information presented in this fashion acts as a reminder.
3. Length is dictated mainly by time for completion. But a questionnaire or schedule shouldn't *look* too lengthy (discouraging) – six A4 pages is probably a maximum.

4. Within that length give questions plenty of space. If the type is small and crowded this will be off-putting; and don't mix up fonts – it'll look too 'busy'.

5. Try to keep one topic (and its questions) to one page: this simple visual organization makes the focus easier for the reader.

6. Ensure that different questions (and their answer formats) are visually distinct from each other. This is partly a matter of spacing but a horizontal separating line across the page helps the process.

7. If you plan to do some follow-up in-depth interviews finish with a request for volunteers: just ticking a 'consent' box is all you need on a questionnaire.

Fine-tuning your method

So far we've talked about development mainly in terms of a questionnaire. It would have been confusing to do otherwise but the content and structure are essentially the same whether you are using:

- a postal questionnaire
- a face-to-face interview (recording schedule)
- a telephone interview.

Which are you going to use? You may decide to use more than one method. If the people you want to question are widely scattered geographically then the face-to-face option is impractical, if not impossible. Where large numbers are involved then interviews are going to be too expensive on time. However, if you want to use physically separate visual material (known as *show cards*) asking, for example, *Which of these do you prefer?* or *Do you know what this logo stands for?* then you need to operate face-to-face.

In any case when making your choice you have to consider the advantages and disadvantages of questionnaires over face-to-face interviews (see Table 9.1).

Table 9.1 Questionnaires and interviews compared

Questionnaires	Face-to-face interviews
• economical on time	• expensive on time
• typically low response rate	• typically high response rate
• large numbers possible	• large numbers impractical
• distance not a problem	• geographical distance limited
• no human interaction	• live interaction
• completion by respondent	• completion by interviewer
• associated problems of data quality	• good data quality
• no control over how they're completed	• control over completion
• misunderstandings cannot be corrected	• misunderstandings easily corrected
• difficult to secure follow-up interviews	• easier to secure follow-up interviews
• requires at least adequate literacy	• negligible literacy requirements

Checking through the table you can see that interviews have the edge *except* when large numbers and/or geographical distance are involved (and telephone interviews can cope with the latter). *With numbers of under 150, interviews are probably to be preferred.* Certainly if numbers are less than 100. There is one powerful argument for this assertion: the fact that a typical response rate to questionnaires is around 30 per cent – so that to get returns of 150 you would have to distribute 500 or so questionnaires and you won't get the balanced sample you are seeking. The exception to this rule is when the questionnaire population is 'captive': in large numbers undergraduates would fit this bill, which is perhaps why they figure so often in studies. People going through a professional training programme are similarly placed and accessible.

Face-to-face interviews (recording schedules)

The questionnaire has been developed to the pilot stage. For interviews you stay with the same content and format. So what's different? In a recording schedule the answers are written/checked by the interviewer on a schedule very much like a questionnaire, designed so as to be quick and unambiguous to record the responses. There are three basic elements:

- the question the interviewer has to ask;
- the prompt to produce a (numbered) show card;
- a simple and quick way of recording the choice of answer, e.g. circling a letter.

So the *design* of the schedule has to fit the way the interview is being conducted. The novel element is the use of *show cards* which you hand to the respondent.

The use of show cards

In a spoken interview it might seem paradoxical to give people cards which they have to read. But the sense of it is clear from an example:

SC1 *Question*: Please look at this card. From **a** to **g** which is your age-range?

a	under 20	**e**	50–59
b	20–29	**f**	60–69
c	30–39	**g**	70 and above
d	40–49		

Note that minimal 'reading' is required (although you can include the question on the card) and that the respondent simply has to indicate the letter. If you read out the choices, with nothing for people to look at, they might 'lose the place' and have to ask you to repeat it.

When an extensive and considered choice is involved then having the choice elements presented simultaneously makes the task easier. For example:

SC2 *Question*: Please look at this card. From **a** to **j** which daily newspaper do you read most often?

a	Sun	**f**	Independent
b	Daily Mail	**g**	Guardian
c	The Times	**h**	Daily Mirror
d	Daily Express	**i**	The Financial Times
e	Daily Telegraph	**j**	Any other: please name

Questions don't always involve show cards, particularly those which are very simple or where the answer(s) cannot be predicted or provided, for example:

Question: Where did you go for your last holiday?

Picture show cards

One of the advantages of a face-to-face interview is that you can present show cards (usually asking for recognition or preference) using a number of them very quickly – because you get a rapid response. Of course visual material can be included in a questionnaire but it can take up a lot of space and it's harder to guide the respondent; nothing simpler than handing someone a show card (or several) and asking: *Which of these do you recognize?* (photographs of cabinet ministers, 'celebrities', advertising logos, etc.).

The choice of material depends on the content and purpose of your research. For example, if the topic is fashion then words alone are going to be quite inadequate. But there is more to it than that: 'visuals' prevent a sense of sameness in the presentation (we've previously emphasized the need to vary question formats).

Images have a distinctive contemporary appeal; and presenting 'visual' questions means tapping into a different dimension of knowledge and judgement.

The telephone interview

Even as I sat down to work on this chapter I was interrupted by a phone call from a 'market researcher': a common sales ploy. I explained that I didn't accept that kind of call. And thereby lies the moral of the tale. Market research/sales calls are a minor but recurring nuisance and this contaminates the use of the telephone to carry out legitimate, i.e. academic, research. Telephone interviewing is not widely used as an academic research tool in the UK; much more so in the US. Its main use is the kind of commercial 'cold call' recounted above. It is a major industry with many books (mainly American) on the subject. As a commentary on the practical operation of capitalism they make chilling reading: particularly those sections that deal with overcoming 'resistance'.

If you are planning to use telephone interviews you need to be alert to this contemporary phenomenon; not least that you put as much distance as possible between yourself and such operations. It is much more than having an appropriate schedule. That's not the difficulty. What we propose is that you use a self-completion questionnaire and talk the respondent through it, having sent it through the post or by email first.

These are the ground rules, which are partly ethical in character:

1. You get the permission of the intended respondent to this kind of interview and explain how you plan to conduct it.
2. You consult their convenience: when would be the best time to ring?
3. You make clear that only a short amount of time is involved: if

they are basically willing then 10 minutes is likely to be considered unexceptionable.

4. You *send* a copy of the questionnaire shortly before the interview time, emphasizing that you are not asking them to do anything before you telephone: they need to approach it fresh (hard to explain why that's important but it is).

5. You seat yourself at a table with your writing hand free and a blank questionnaire for recording their answers (*you* do it, not them).

Once you've piloted the procedure (next chapter), it is a comparatively simple exercise. If you have a couple of 'open' questions towards the end you may find yourself scribbling away but, at that stage, it hardly interrupts the flow. Of course you can conduct longer, more loosely structured, more in-depth interviews by telephone but these involve special recording equipment, and are usually at the qualitative end of research interviewing (see Chapter 14 in Gillham 2005).

In some ways the telephone interview is the ultimate test of all the preparation you have engaged in. But we are not finished with that yet. The piloting stage doesn't just test out the schedule, it also rehearses how it is going to be used.

10

The Piloting Stage

Piloting is a simulation of the main study, carried out under the same conditions, so that you can learn any last-minute lessons before sending off 500 questionnaires or doing 100 interviews. Preparation does not guarantee success but is nonetheless indispensable. Developing a new car takes years of design and testing work; but in road-trialling of a prototype it can emerge that it threatens to overturn when cornering at normal speed.

We can expect nothing so dramatic as that. Yet however far-fetched the analogy it focuses the mind on the importance of the unaided piloting stage: how your questionnaire operates under real-life conditions.

So much development has gone into it. The question is: will it run?

The purpose of the pilot

What do you hope to learn? Three things:

- whether the *content* of the interview or questionnaire needs any changes;
- whether, as a whole, it *works* as intended;
- whether the stage of *analysis* throws up any difficulties.

The last point is one we have scarcely touched on, and there may be something to take from it. If you have open questions in the questionnaire you may well find the content analysis is more problematic and takes longer than expected; and if that's true at the pilot stage it will be even more so in the main study. Perhaps you get a pattern of responses to one of the items in the questionnaire that indicates the question is being understood in a quite different way from the one you intended. In total the pilot is a 'dress rehearsal' for the real thing – in all its components.

How many people should be involved?

If a questionnaire is your choice then around 20 to 30; and about five if you plan to use a recording schedule or telephone interview. Even with the modest numbers indicated this involves a substantial amount of work but it makes a significant contribution to the smooth running of the main study. Better to correct things now as they show up, and if they don't then you have that reassurance.

Piloting a questionnaire

Of all the survey instruments we are considering this is the one that has to undergo the toughest test. You have to launch the questionnaire: which then stands on its own. You won't be able to clarify or correct it. So how will you know if things are not going to plan?

The first thing to alert you is a slow or very low response rate. A 'troublesome' questionnaire is a low priority for most people (if it is a priority at all). And when you scrutinize the returned questionnaires you should look out for 'misunderstandings' which will show themselves in a variety of ways:

- omitted responses;
- incomplete, crossed-out or ? responses;

- frequent comments like N/A or don't know/not sure or extra points or categories added to the answer format.

A key indicator is when several people have had difficulty with the *same* question; it may be that the design/layout of the questionnaire is at fault.

There is another possibility arising out of the difficulties noted above: that maybe you should use an interview rather than a questionnaire to gather your data. Unless you get a good response rate (50 per cent plus) and the questions are working well, then that alternative has to be considered.

The recording schedule variant

Being face-to-face is a great advantage: you can anticipate problems and see when something is not working as it should. And if you find you have to reword or supplement questions the implications are obvious. But much of what you'll learn here is in the practical 'rehearsal' aspect. In a phrase: have you got your act together? It is easy to get flustered if you are interviewing people in the street. Can you fluently produce your show cards while prompting them with the question-and-answer choice? Are your 'open' questions difficult to record? Is it all taking too long? Your first one or two attempts probably will but if it's still the case with the fifth person then you may have to consider further pruning of the content – or simplifying the procedure.

Arranging a telephone interview

'Telephone awkwardness' is largely a thing of the past: people talk as easily on their mobile as they do in person. But that's in the informal mode and usually with people they know well: telephone interviewing is quite different. 'Formal' interviewing is a complex skill which requires focused attention on the interviewee, particularly in an unstructured interview where you have to attend closely to the interviewee's responses – and much of this is non-verbal. In a telephone interview (at least at present) that visual dimension is missing, as well as that person-to-person chemistry which is so difficult to define.

But here we are considering a highly structured interview: in effect the assisted completion of a postal questionnaire. You arrange a time for the call, sending the questionnaire in advance, and then talk the respondents through it, recording the responses on *your* copy so that they don't have to return theirs.

What advantages does this have over simply sending a questionnaire for them to complete? Twofold:

- it is more likely to be completed;
- *you* have control of the process and can deal with hesitations or misunderstandings.

By sending the hard copy to your respondents they can see what they are letting themselves in for; and with the text in front of them they don't have to strain attention to what is coming through the ether. Most people find this less of a challenge than having to fill in a questionnaire on their own.

Again you will have to check on the time involved. Fifteen minutes is probably a maximum: ten is what you should aim for.

Reviewing the pilot

Unless you have gone astray in the earlier stages of development, the lessons from the piloting phase will be relatively minor – and almost self-evident. But you need to take time to review the findings: checking through the completed questionnaires and interview schedules with a blank version so you can mark necessary changes. Not difficult but not unimportant.

However, there is one problem which only really shows up at this stage, and that is how long it takes to complete the questionnaire in its interview schedule format. In the earlier stages of trialling we were dealing only with the questionnaire and often interrupting the process to get feedback. So the wider issue of duration had been put to one side.

If you find now that your recording schedule, where you've been interviewing people on the hoof in the street, has averaged 15 minutes then that is definitely too long. Even at this late stage major pruning is going to be necessary. With all the development work behind you it can be hard to let go; but it is likely that another topic section will have to be deleted. Quite simply you take something off the bottom of the list – the lowest priority – even if you feel the content is desirable for your research.

Controlling the length of interviews is important even when they are being conducted in relative comfort and at a modest pace. As in writing, pruning always improves focus. The leaner and fitter it is, the better your schedule will stay the course; and the analysis stage will be less punishing. This last is something you won't have done before so there is a good deal to learn from it: not least the amount of work you may be letting yourself in for.

The details of analysis are given in Chapters 12, 13 and 14 so you will have to go forward in the text for that purpose. But it is not enough just to read those chapters through: you have to practise the techniques *using the data from the pilot study*. Any practical activity only becomes clear in action so it is a kind of rehearsal; it also shows up weaknesses in question-and-answer formats. Problems of analysis usually stem from faults in the way the 'task' has been presented to the respondent – and these weaknesses may not be evident in other ways.

11

Running the Main Study

You have a well-developed product, now it's a matter of seeing how the 'market' will respond to it. This is more of a problem with questionnaires than with interviews so we'll deal with those first.

Getting them out and getting them back

This inelegant heading nonetheless encapsulates the problem. Sending out questionnaires is one thing; getting them back quite another. The following guidelines take it for granted that you have a well-designed questionnaire.

- Questionnaires that are personally delivered (and to people you know) have the best chance of being returned.
- A personal appeal in the sense of saying *why* you are doing the research (as part of a Master's degree, for example) will also encourage a response: people will understand that it is important to you.
- Sponsorship and identity: showing where you are coming from is also helpful. If your research is being carried out in the context of a university or similar institution then you need to say so – preferably via appropriately headed paper. If a postal questionnaire goes out through the university postal system, i.e. franked, that will also reinforce your identity. The

independence and status of universities are well-recognized so your request will be taken more seriously.

- In a covering letter address the recipient personally, being careful to get name, initials and title correct – and *sign* the letter. At this point you might ask: what about email? Easy to send, yes, but it lacks a number of qualities important for survey purposes (confidentiality, distinctiveness, how it is to be returned, the 'personal' dimension). It has also to be said that email can have something like junk-mail status (*I've had 60 emails today*): you have to make sure that your questionnaire rises above that.

- Enclose a stamped addressed envelope – much more likely to get a reply (as mail-order companies appreciate). You should do this even if you have hand-delivered the original questionnaire. Post-mail is still the simplest confidential way of sending such material.

Enhancing returns

After a predictable pause for delivery, completion and return, a useful rule of thumb is that the number returned within ten days is about half the final figure to be returned *provided that you follow-up assiduously*. A neglected questionnaire is soon consigned to the waste-paper basket. So you need to do your follow-up pretty quickly: two weeks after the initial mailing is about right. You should send a further copy of the questionnaire 'in case they did not receive or have mislaid the original' together with a stamped addressed envelope. It should be accompanied by a short letter which:

- is not apologetic (irritating);
- emphasizes the importance of the study and *their contribution*;
- doesn't imply you've had a poor response (imply the contrary, if anything).

You can expect quite a good response to that. But wait another ten days and then send a further *brief* follow-up letter (but not reproachful – irritating again). This may bring a few more returns but by then it is wise to leave well alone.

However, if the response rate is still low you might have to make the difficult decision to switch to an interview approach. There is nothing to be ashamed of in this: real-life research is like that. Such a decision should be recorded in your research report; together with a consideration of the probable reasons for the poor questionnaire uptake. And it will not be wasted as you can do a comparison of the data from the different sources.

Face-to-face interviews: planning your programme

A well-honed recording schedule is quick to administer and surprisingly interesting, highly structured though it is. If you enjoy dealing with people this is the most attractive of the methods we describe. But it demands intense concentration (true of all interviews) and can be very tiring, particularly if you have to stand in the street juggling all your materials at speed. A simple calculation might suggest that you could do ten 10-minute interviews in a couple of hours. In practice it takes longer than that for reasons too obvious to detail.

Don't try to do more than six to ten interviews in one half-day session. Your concentration and energy are soon used up so that your administration takes on a mechanical quality. The under-graduate described on pages 23–4 averaged twenty a day; but we don't all have her stamina and dynamism. The quality of what you get from the people you interview is something to do with the freshness and interest you bring to these very short interviews.

In any case, each day you should check through the schedules you've completed (any mistakes on your part?), and record briefly your description and impressions of how the day's work has gone. An undemanding way of doing this is to audio-record your thoughts (which will form part of your research data). Contemporaneous notes can be vivid but also encourage reflection. Remember that no research method is perfect and

71

part of the process (as in a higher degree thesis) is learning *how* to do research – so that writing up what you've learnt is part of a whole account. This kind of daily self-commentary is lost if you just focus on increasing your score of schedules completed: all that remains is some kind of impression, lacking in detail and specificity.

The structured telephone interview

We need to reiterate the point that time spent setting these up pays dividends in terms of quality.

A primary consideration is consulting people's convenience. Even if you have agreed a time and date you should check whether that is *still* convenient. Busy people are subject to unpredictable levels of demand: make a new appointment if necessary. Check that they have received the copy of the schedule. If you want to send illustrative material then incorporate it in the schedule (not on entirely separate show cards). In general, keep this sort of thing to a minimum *unless* visuals are the main focus of the interview.

Bear in mind that telephone interviews are uniquely tiring (something about the level of concentration required), particularly for the interviewer. And if tiredness/staleness shows in your voice this will be communicated because all the respondent has to go on is your voice quality. If you try to do more than two an hour then the effect will be marked; one hour when you also record your impressions as well as taking a break is a relatively easy pace that nonetheless covers the ground.

One final detail in relation to telephone interviews is what is sometimes referred to as *social closure*. In a face-to-face interview this occurs almost without reflection or prompting: expressing your thanks and appreciation, a smile and a handshake, where there is a quality of gradualness because of the 'live' character of the interaction. At the end of a telephone interview it is too easy to put the phone down in a way which can seem abrupt; how you express your appreciation is up to you but it does require conscious attention, a little effort – not an apparent 'now that's over' message.

Completing your sample

People respond better to interviews than to questionnaires, but you can still get refusals and, if you are working to a quota sample, this may take longer than you expect. Quota sample interviewing requires persistence; when all your quota categories are open then filling them does not seem a problem, but as the categories fill up, the remaining gaps are slower to complete. You need to keep this under review, so if you're doing a street-sited survey, keep a tally of the grouping of the people you've interviewed. It's easy to lose sight of the wider picture and such a tally alerts you to 'gaps' in your sample so you know whom you should be looking for. In the case of telephone interviews it is useful to have a supplementary list which you can turn to as necessary.

It may seem that doing a piece of research is a series of hurdles: you're got over that one – but what's in front of you? Certainly *data-collection* is the biggest challenge. The mistake is to think that when that's accomplished you're home and dry. The two further hurdles are:

- analysing the data;
- writing up your findings.

The latter is a book-length topic in its own right and, curiously, one where people often stall. Pulling the whole thing together is an intellectually demanding business. The consolation is that your careful preparation and well organized analysis will make it a good deal easier.

12

Descriptive Data Analysis

Accumulating data is largely a practical problem, not a particularly intellectual one. The intellectual challenge is to make sense of the material. The first task is to see what exactly has been collected: setting out the data in such a way that you can move on to the second phase – *interpreting the findings*. Analysis is, therefore, dependent on a thoughtful and well-organized display of the data, which will, in turn, help you understand what you've got and where this information will lead you.

The importance of this stage of research is often underestimated. In the history of science it is the grand theorists who get the most credit. Darwin said you cannot observe without a theory; but prior descriptive classification makes theory-driven observation possible. Darwin couldn't have achieved what he did without the painstaking classificatory systems of the plant and animal kingdom, of flora and fauna, developed by the eighteenth-century Swedish naturalist Linnaeus, or the early nineteenth-century French scientist Lamarck's work on species evolution.

When carrying out research you come to know it better as one stage succeeds another; you learn something new at each point. Organizing and displaying continues that process and, as we shall see, the act of interpreting and writing up – the effort of making coherent sense – leads to further insights. You don't see it all at once.

Graphical display of responses to closed questions

Although there are several ways of dealing with the limited range of responses to closed questions, essentially it is quite a simple exercise: you count the answers that have been checked, prepare numerical tables and then convert these into diagrams.

Displays that are easy to read are of two main kinds: bar graphs and pie charts. They are much more accessible than numerical tables or line graphs, and superior to any attempts – other than the most elementary comparisons – to detailing the data in words. Words are good for picking out distinctive features of the data and emphasizing them, with charts or graphs illustrating the emphasis. That is part of the interpretive process (see Chapter 15).

Different kinds of closed questions

Basically we have two kinds of questions: First those that 'describe' the people who have completed the questionnaire or interview, in terms of gender, age and so on – categories chosen because of their probable relevance to the second kind of question, those that deal with the main topics of the research. The subject descriptor variables enable us to divide up the answers to the research topic questions to see whether there are any differences of interest. It should be said that the subject descriptors should not be chopped too finely, especially if numbers are not large. In part this is so that statistical differences can be calculated with a chance of reaching a level of significance.

So a first stage is to display the characteristics of the people in your survey group according to the descriptors you've chosen (age, income, educational attainment, etc.). You can then see how the numbers fall and what kind of simpler division would better reflect the differences in the group. Note that in Figure 12.1 we have collapsed some of the educational level categories given on p. 44 and could do so even more, depending on the importance of

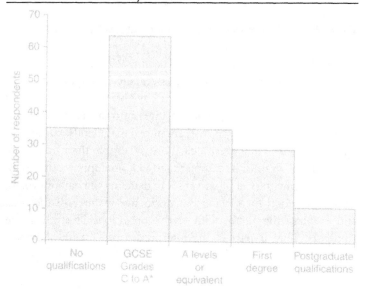

Figure 12.1 Example of a subject descriptor bar graph (highest level of educational attainment)

the distinctions and how far it makes sense to subdivide the data. For example, we could put the data into two categories, below degree level, and degree level and above. At this point you can start to see where important differences might lie. It depends on what sort of group you are dealing with: for juveniles who have made a first court appearance, for example, the 'no qualifications' category would likely be larger – and more significant.

Getting a clearer picture of your sample

Pie charts provide another way of illustrating a sample. If it was decided to reduce the age-range categories into those aged under 45, and those aged 45 and over, then you could do it as in Figure 12.2.

Pie charts are a vivid way of demonstrating simple comparisons particularly if you use colour. They work best when there are not

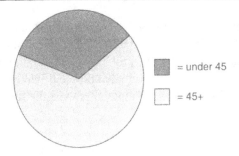

Figure 12.2 Pie chart showing age proportions of sample

too many slices to the pie (about four or five is a maximum). For more than that bar graphs work better; where some differences are very small the vertical bar comparisons make this distinction easier to see.

Pie charts side by side are particularly effective when you want to demonstrate a marked difference between two groups (as in Figure 12.3).

It is not suggested that you shouldn't include numerical tables in your research report; exact numbers are not easy to read in a diagram, although you can enter these in the relevant bar or pie slice perhaps including a percentage as well, e.g. 63 (40%). In addition, if you are going to carry out a statistical analysis (see Chapter 13) then the data have to be in numerical form.

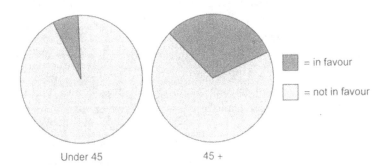

Figure 12.3 Proportions in favour of the physical punishment of children under the age of five, by age of sample

Even this basic descriptive exercise, carried out across the different subject descriptor variables, will enable you to see more clearly what kind of sample you have, and how and where it might be broken down. The subdivisions can then be set against the pattern of answers to the topic questions: the 'meat' of your survey.

Analysing the answers

Here the process is similar to analysing the subject descriptor details but slightly more complicated. You need an A4 sheet in landscape orientation with the question written along the top and the answer categories across the page underneath, perhaps further subdivided in the left-hand column by one of your subject descriptor categories, as shown in Tables 12.1 and 12.2. This saves further work because you can still see the totals within each answer category but you start to see where significant differences within them might be found.

However you have framed your subject descriptor questions, i.e. five age-groups, as many income groups, it is usually better to collapse these with a sufficient number in each group for statistical processing. But you don't know where that division is best placed until all the data have been gathered in. The same applies when you have several answer categories (see Table 12.2).

With very large numbers of people surveyed (and many topics/questions/answers) it can be useful to have each answer choice coded, i.e. assigned a unique number. A 150-answer questionnaire would therefore have them numbered 1 to 150, and you can see that the data set could present problems of management, perhaps requiring the use of specialist software. In small-scale surveys that can be too abstract and complicated. What is proposed here is that, taking your A4 sheets (one to a question) you work across the questionnaires putting a check mark for each answer chosen. Table 12.1 takes an example from p. 39.

A slightly more complicated example (using hypothetical data

Table 12.1 Distribution of answers by age

The Health Centre provides a very good appointments service
(TICK ONE BOX)

Age group	Agree	Not sure	Disagree	Strongly disagree
45+	₩₩ ₩₩ ₩₩ (15)	₩₩ ₩₩ (10)	₩₩ ₩₩ (10)	₩₩ I (6)
Under 45	₩₩ ₩₩ ₩₩ ₩₩ III (23)	III (3)	₩₩ III (8)	(0)
Total	38	13	18	6

from answers given to the questions on p. 37) is shown in Table
12.2.

Table 12.2 Distribution of answers by gender

Which aspect of the weight-control programme did you find most
useful? Put 1 against what you found **most** useful, 2 against the
next most useful and so on down to 5 for the **least** useful.

	(a) Scientific information		(b) Fallacies about dieting		(c) Advice on healthy eating		(d) Information on unhealthy eating		(e) Changing exercise patterns	
	1/2	4/5	1/2	4/5	1/2	4/5	1/2	4/5	1/2	4/5
M	₩₩ ₩₩ II (12)	III (3)	₩₩ ₩₩ II (12)	₩₩ III (8)	₩₩ ₩₩ II (12)	₩₩ III (8)	IIII (4)	₩₩ ₩₩ ₩₩ (15)	₩₩ III (8)	₩₩ ₩₩ III (13)
F	₩₩ III (8)	₩₩ III (8)	₩₩ ₩₩ III (13)	₩₩ I (6)	₩₩ III (8)	₩₩ IIII (14)	₩₩ ₩₩ II (12)	₩₩(5)	₩₩ ₩₩ III (13)	₩₩ II (7)
Total	20	11	25	14	20	22	16	20	21	20

Note that we have collapsed the two categories at each end
(1+2 and 4+5) and discarded the 3 rating, for purposes of
emphasis and, perhaps, later statistical analysis.

Topic questions: displaying the results

The results as shown in Tables 12.1 and 12.2 are not easy to see.
They need a more visual form of display.

If we compare the bar graph (Figure 12.4) with Table 12.1 the

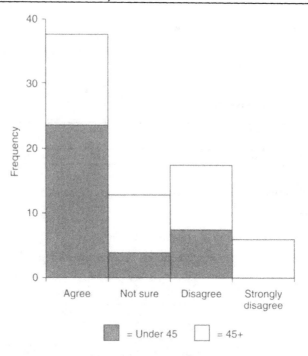

Figure 12.4 Data from Table 12.1 in bar graph format

impact (and simplicity) of the 'visuality' dimension is evident, as are the *apparent* differences between the two groups (under 45 and 45+).

Seeing any pattern is even more difficult in Table 12.2. How could this be displayed graphically? There are two sets of data here. Different *aspects* of the programme are rated *high* or *low* – irrespective of differences in the subjects. And then differences between ratings according to *gender* – do any of these look significant? We need to prepare separate bar graphs for each aspect of the programme: as shown in Figure 12.5.

The bar graph display shows some interesting difference's between the subject groups: for example in category (d) (information on unhealthy eating) we get an almost exactly reversed picture for the two sexes – much more striking as displayed here than as a set of tally marks. For analysis these are best presented

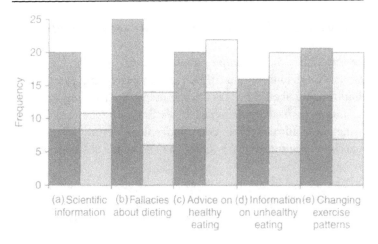

Figure 12.5 Data from Table 12.2

as a 2×2 numerical table (Table 12.3).

Table 12.3 Gender differences in rating of item (d), as shown in Table 12.2

	High	Low	Total
M	4	15	19
F	12	5	17
Total	16	20	N = 36

This table is ready for the application of the statistic *chi square* (χ^2) – explained in Chapter 13 – to see whether the gender difference is significant. By selecting this, the most marked difference, we shall also be able to judge whether other less marked gender differences might be worth analysing in this fashion.

Significant differences: what are we looking for?

Description is never simple; nor is 'seeing'. We don't just take what is there in front of us. Much of it confirms what we expect to find, but we should be alert to the unexpected. In any case our assumptions need challenging. If we think we 'see' a difference (whether confirming our prior judgement or not) we need to check out the status of the 'difference'. Couldn't it have occurred by chance?

The answer is that *any* difference can occur by chance; and the necessary calculation is what that likelihood amounts to. Here we are stepping into *probability theory*, which soon becomes deep water.

If we look back at Table 12.3 the reverse order difference in the ratings given by men and women is readily apparent. But if, for example, the figures had read:

	High	*Low*
M	9	10
F	9	8

– where the same numbers of men and women are evenly balanced then we wouldn't give them a second glance. However, if the figures were in extreme opposition:

	High	*Low*
M	19	0
F	0	17

– we should be very intrigued.

But what Table 12.3 shows is an in-between (though still quite marked) difference. Exactly how do we explore that?

13

Statistical Analysis

It may be that you are perfectly comfortable with mathematics and that subsection known as statistics. If so you are fortunate, and in a minority; many students take fright at the very mention of the term. Ability in mathematics is definitely a particular kind of intelligence. The trouble is that people with this aptitude often cannot see what the problem is for others: to them it is either obvious (!) or an exciting challenge. Being myself of an in-between status I have some understanding of both sides of the issue.

Here we are only dealing with one simple test which nonetheless can give a degree of precision to an impressionistic judgement of a categorical difference in the data.

The computation of chi square (χ^2)

In the previous chapter we saw how Table 12.3 showed an apparent difference in response to item (d) in a weight-control programme. The actual figures are given in a 2×2 *contingency table* – so called because one variable (High or Low rating) is contingent on the other (in this case *gender*).

The *chi square* test (the *chi* stands for the Greek letter χ - hence χ^2) deals with categorical data like these and enables us to say something definite about the disparities between different categories. You might feel that the results speak for themselves without any statistical manipulation. There *is* a numerical difference, but what does it amount to? The numbers involved are not large and surely the occasional difference of this kind is only to be expected? On the other hand, by impression alone you might claim a difference that could easily have arisen by chance. What this kind of test does is tell us *how likely* it is to be a chance result.

If it is shown to be unlikely, there may be something which requires further exploratory research.

The rationale of chi square

The basic premise is simple: in Table 12.3 we have the actual or *obtained* frequencies. We then make a comparison with the frequencies that would be *expected* if there were no difference between men and women.

Of the total number of respondents involved (36) 16 rated *information on unhealthy eating* as a very useful component of the weight-control programme: that is 44.44 per cent. If there were no difference between men and women we would expect the same percentage in each case to rate that programme component highly but this is not so (see Table 13.1).

Table 13.1 Comparison between obtained and expected frequencies

	Obtained		Expected	
	High	Low	High	Low
M	4 [21.0%]	15 [79.0%]	8.44 [44.44%]	10.56 [55.56%]
F	12 [70.6%]	5 [29.4%]	7.55 [44.44%]	9.45 [55.56%]

On the left are the *obtained* frequencies and on the right the *expected* frequencies. The difference between the frequencies for each cell (o − e) is the basis of chi square. This is what we have to keep in mind as we go through the various steps in the calculation. (NB The percentages are shown here for illustration; we don't use them in the actual calculation of chi square.)

Step 0

If you were able to follow the previous section without difficulty then you can skip this expanded explanation. But experience shows that many aspirants fall at the first hurdle, so here goes . . .

- To recap: the basis of chi square is the *difference* between the frequencies (i.e. how many) actually *obtained* and what we should *expect* if the pattern of responses were the same for the two groups.
- We use chi square when it looks as if there might be a significant difference, as shown in Table 12.3, where the *obtained* frequencies certainly look very different for men and women rating the information on unhealthy eating – almost a reverse picture in fact.
- The total for *all* the cells (and so 100%) is 36. Of this total 16 people (M+F) rated the item (d) as *high* while 20 people (M+F) rated it as *low* (Table 12.2). That is, 44.44% high rating ($\frac{16}{36} \times 100$) and 55.56% low rating ($\frac{20}{36} \times 100$).
- If there were no gender differences in response we should get the same *percentage* in each case (actual numbers not the same – 19 men and 17 women – but chi square can cope with that).
- So, the 'no difference' *expected* frequencies for men would be 8.44 high rating (44.44% of 19) and 10.56 low rating (55.56% of 19). For women they would be 7.55 high rating (44.44% of 17) and 9.45 low rating (55.56% of 17).

A computer program like *SPSS* (*Statistical Program for the Social Services*) could do all this for you, but it is necessary to understand what's involved if this is your first encounter with chi square, and a basic calculator is quite adequate for the computation.

Step 1

For each cell calculate the difference between the obtained frequency (o) and the expected frequency (e), expressed as (o − e). This gives us:

− 4.44	+ 4.44
+ 4.45	− 4.45

Some numbers are negative (because we are taking a larger number from a smaller one) but it is the *size* of the difference, not its direction that is important.

Step 2

The next step is to square the differences $(o - e)^2$ which has the effect of getting rid of the negative signs, as follows:

19.71	19.71
19.80	19.80

Step 3

Each number is divided by the *expected* frequency for that cell: $(o - e)^2 \div e$. For example, for the first cell in the first row we calculate $19.71 \div 8.44 = 2.34$ and so on. Which gives us:

2.34	1.87
2.62	2.10

Step 4

The sum of these is the value of $\chi^2 = 8.93$.

To find out if this is statistically significant we can consult a table of chi square values (to be found in the appendices of statistical texts).

Note that in order to read off the significance level of chi square we have to calculate the *degrees of freedom* for the 2×2 contingency table.

The formula for calculating degrees of freedom (df) is:

$(r - 1) \times (k - 1)$

where:

r = number of rows

k = number of columns

So in our 2×2 contingency table we have:

$(2 - 1) \times (2 - 1)$

$= 1 \times 1 = 1$ df

What this means is that when one cell has been determined, all the others have to fit to it: they have no 'freedom'.

Since we have just 1 df our task is straightforward; for more than this the chi square values are different. The following table is taken from Greene and d'Oliviera 1999, p. 212.

Table 13.2 Significance levels for different values of χ^2

	p values				
df	0.10	0.05	0.02	0.01	0.001
1	2.71	3.84	5.41	6.64	10.83

We can see that a χ^2 value of 8.93 with one degree of freedom falls between a *p* value of 0.01 and 0.001. But what does '*p value*' mean?

1. *p* stands for 'probability'.
2. Probability is most easily understood in terms of how often (1 in 10, 1 in 100, etc.) a given result could occur by chance.
3. To put it another way, the rarer the event, the greater the probability that it is significant.
4. Statisticians talk about 'levels of significance' in these terms except that they are expressed as a decimal of 1.0 which is a more economical way of doing so. Hence, in the table from Greene and d'Oliviera's book (which is recommended for

consultation), p values are given as 0.10, 0.05 and so on. Conventionally the 0.05 (1 chance in 20) level is the *minimum* regarded as significant. With shorter odds, for example:

0.50 = 5 chances in 10, or 1 chance in 2 (evens)
0.10 = 1 chance in 10

– you don't need to be a mathematical genius to appreciate that these are hardly significant: they could very easily have occurred by chance.

But the following are conventionally regarded as more or less significant:

0.05 = 5 chances in 100 or 1 chance in 20
0.01 = 1 chance in 100
0.001 = 1 chance in 1,000

and so on.

It is one thing to read an explanation: to really understand it you have to be able to carry out the procedure yourself. Try the following exercise (answers at the end of the chapter):

What are the probabilities for these significance levels?

0.25　　= 1 chance in _____
0.20　　= 1 chance in _____
0.02　　= 1 chance in _____
0.005　 = 1 chance in _____
0.002　 = 1 chance in _____
0.0001 = 1 chance in _____

Apart from looking up the answers there is a simple way of checking whether you are correct. Can you see it? Again, the answer is given at the end of the chapter.

Once you are clear as to what a p value is we can look at our χ^2 result (p. 86) in relation to Greene and d'Oliviera's table. Because $\chi^2 = 8.93$ falls between the $p = 0.01$ value (6.64) and the 0.001 value (10.83) we can claim it as highly significant, and hazard a guess that it could only have occurred about once in 500 by chance. If these were actual data (which they are not) we should then be left with the intriguing question of *why* there is a gender difference in rating the usefulness of information about unhealthy eating.

A practical exercise

Having found one highly significant difference between the sexes in the data in Table 12.2 (p. 79) we might want to look at some of the other differences. Initially we had picked the most obvious; but what about column (e) *Changing exercise patterns?* Note that if we hadn't carved up the results in terms of gender they would look very evenly balanced (21 'high rating', 20 'low rating'). With gender taken into account we get the distribution shown in Table 13.3.

Table 13.3 Distribution of ratings by gender

	High	Low	Total
M	8	13	21
F	13	7	20
Total	21	20	N = 41

Following the procedure given on pp. 85–6 calculate chi square: does it reach a conventional level of significance? (answer at the end of the chapter).
Why is it important to calculate the significance of differences?

It is one thing to show (or describe) your findings, it is quite another to draw inferences from them: this is the difference between *descriptive* and *inferential* statistics. The kind of test we have described is widely applicable to questionnaire data that fall into categories. You are bound to notice differences but what do you make of them? Look back at the data in Table 12.1 (p. 79) which uses an *agree/not sure/disagree/strongly disagree* scale, i.e. weighted towards critical judgements with the aim of improving the Health Centre's appointments system. The data are divided by age group; if we disregard the 'not sure' category and combine the disagree/strongly disagree categories we find the following:

Table 13.4 Distribution of levels of agreement by age category

	Agree	Disagree	Total
45+	15	16	31
Under 45	23	8	31
Total	38	24	N = 62

By this time you will have 'got your eye in' for this kind of table: does it look significant? Calculate it and see if it is (answer at the end of the chapter).

A final caution

A ranking scale (as in Table 12.2) where the responses are in terms of numbers (1 for most useful to 5 least useful) invites a procedure which is not legitimate. For example, in category (a) of that table we may have obtained the following frequencies for the different ranks (shown in Table 13.5).

Table 13.5 Usefulness rating of scientific information component in weight management programme, as shown in Table 12.2(a).

	Rating					
	1	2	3	4	5	Total
M	5	7	6	2	1	21
F	3	5	4	5	3	20
Total	8	12	10	7	4	41

Note that the ratings are 1 to 5; the figures underneath are the number of people who gave that rating.

When you are dealing with 'number' ratings rather than 'word' ratings – for example 1 (high) to 5 (low) – it is tempting to think that you can *average* the ratings as if they were scores, e.g. the 'average' for men is 2.38, the 'average' for women is 3.00, and so on. But this implies that the difference between the points of the rating scale are equal (as on an *interval* scale like centimetres). Here the numbers are merely a way of giving the order of the ratings – an *ordinal* scale. Put simply, the numbers mean no more than words (like *high* to *low*) – and words cannot be averaged. Whether you are persuaded is another matter ...

Exercise answers

P. 88

Probabilities: 0.25   = 1 chance in 4
                0.20   = 1 chance in 5
                0.02   = 1 chance in 50
                0.005   = 1 chance in 200
                0.002   = 1 chance in 500
                0.0001 = 1 chance in 10,000

Checking your answers: the decimal multiplied by the level of chance should equal 1.0 (0.25 × 4; 0.005 × 200, and so on).

P. 89 *(Table 13.3)*

$\chi^2 = 2.97$. Is that significant? Consult significance table on p. 87.

P. 90 *(Table 13.4)*

$\chi^2 = 4.34$. How significant is that? Consult significance table on p. 87.

14

Content Analysis

Content analysis involves putting your data (content) into descriptive categories. In this case putting the answers to open questions into categories relevant to your research purpose – what it is that you want to find out.

So-called 'classic' content analysis was first used to categorize the content of newspapers (measured in column inches) with so much devoted to foreign news, sport, the arts and so on. That remains a technique of interest and is appealingly simple because not much interpretation of the material is involved. When the material to be analysed is not so standard it soon becomes a more complicated exercise. In that case you have to *derive* or infer the categories from the data and this is a matter of judgement: there is no one 'right' set of categories.

The use of computers

It would be pleasant to think that computers could take over the donkey work of analysis. The trouble is that you have first to make sense of your own unique set of data. Once you have done that it is possible to use appropriate software to store and organize it. The best known is *NVivo* for qualitative data, though for small-scale studies it is hardly necessary. Major research programmes will often have their own specially designed software.

The most useful are likely to be office-type software (*Microsoft Word* and *Excel* for spreadsheets) which will enable you to set out your data after the basic analysis. Computers have human intelligence beaten when it comes to the storage, organization and accurate retrieval of large amounts of information; but as far as judgement and interpretation (especially of meaning) are concerned then they are vastly inferior, as is evident in computer-based 'translations'.

The analysis of open questions

To recap: an 'open' question is one where the range of answers is open – and may be unpredictable. However, when the *kind* of answer is exactly specified there isn't much difference from a closed question. For example, an appropriate question on educational qualifications in England and Wales might be:

What A levels do you have and what grades did you get?

Please list:

	Subject	Grade
1.		
2.		
3.		
4.		
5.		

This is called a *specified response* question and because the range of possible answers is large, setting it out in this fashion is the only economical way of doing it. You can then describe and analyse the results as you see fit (proportion at grades A or B; whether a foreign language is included; proportion of science subjects, etc.).

This sort of analysis of content is straightforward and doesn't need to be spelt out.

Degrees of openness

If you are carrying out the kind of extended interviews where you are using 'wide open' questions (*What was it like to be made redundant?*), following up and exploring the responses (see the Gillham (2000) *The Research Interview*) you will get some rich and interesting material. But seeing the commonalities (potential categories) and analysing it in those terms is likely to be difficult, even if you only have a dozen or so interview transcripts to deal with.

However, if you have included a couple of wide-open questions in a questionnaire that yields 200 returns you have a very difficult task, unless you are experienced and expert in the use of categorical software (and it's easy to get lost in that).

We have suggested that you carry out a practice analysis of your data at the piloting stage: what you encounter there may well indicate the need to modify your questions, in particular to close the degree of openness. For example, you might have drafted the question:

What are your views on the use of email?

You could close this up a bit by asking:

What do you see as the positive and negative features of email?

Closer still you could ask:

What do you see as the three most positive and the three most negative features of email?

It is not difficult to see that the last of these would be the easiest to analyse. But every constraint loses something. I use the second of these with post-graduate students in the form:

What do you see as the positive and negative features of your course?

The reason for choosing this rather than the 'tightest' option (three positives and three negatives) is that you lose something important. Typically more negatives come up than positives; and they are more diverse. But it is these negatives that indicate what requires corrective attention. I also use this as an exercise with the students in carrying out a categorical content analysis. I photocopy the entire set and then get the students to classify them in spreadsheet format, e.g.:

Respondent	Category		
	A	B	C etc.
1			
2			
3 etc.			

Although differently expressed there are usually broad commonalities. I then photocopy their analyses so they can see that though there are similarities in their categories and how they are labelled, it is a matter of interpretation (and therefore 'subjective'). There are no 'objective' categories: such a function is a property of the human mind, even if objective criteria are given.

You could carry out a similar exercise yourself – easy if you are part of a group working for a particular degree.

A further exercise

Content analysis is a process that cannot be understood simply by reading a book like this. To understand what is written here you have to practise the technique. The most difficult part is the formation of categories: and you will only really *see* what's in your data when you've done this.

The first stage is to identify *substantive* statements, i.e. those that say something of substance, that reflect an attitude. In the following (fictional) data my selections are in square brackets; you may not agree but neither of us is right or wrong, it's a matter of subjective judgement.

Question: What is your attitude to what is usually called 'junk mail'?

Responses:

a.   Depends what you mean by attitude: I suppose I just feel a kind of boredom. [Don't give it a second thought.]

b.   No one seems to have a good word to say for it but, well, I don't get so much mail so I shuffle through it and [sometimes I find something of interest – especially in catalogues: for the garden, things like that].

c.   [It depends what it is] I don't like the sorts of envelopes that say: *Personally hand-delivered for the attention of the occupier.* Do they think you're stupid?

d.   If it says *Private and confidential* I bin it: it can't be all that private and confidential. [Occasionally something attracts my attention.]

e.   [I feel sorry for the postman having to cart all that stuff around,] even if it does earn the Post Office money.

f.   [Extreme irritation. I never give it any attention]. After all, if it was so worthwhile they wouldn't have to go to all that trouble promoting it, whatever it is.

g.   [I don't read anything that offers bargain insurance quotations.] Insurance is a bit of a racket anyway.

h.   Depends how busy I am: at the weekend or on holiday [I might spend an idle ten minutes on it].

i.   It must cost the advertiser a fortune – so [what's the real worth of what they're promoting?]

j.   [It's a mixture isn't it?] [I bought some very nice garden bulbs that way – winter aconites – quite hard to find.]

k.   I know a lot of people buy on the internet or whatever but I haven't got a computer and it's a bit of a trek to the shops. It's just like everything else [you have to make up your own mind. I mean there's nobody there *forcing* you to buy something, is there?]

If you read these comments through you can see that some of the things said are similar, but sorting them into categories is another matter. Whichever statements you identify, the next stage is to derive *possible* categories you might put them into. (You're not actually putting them in the categories at this point.) In some ways this is the most difficult stage of all. The trick is not to make the categories too narrow or you end up with each statement having its own category. Here's my attempt to identify common themes:

1. Ignored
2. Occasionally read
3. Occasionally useful
4. Doubts about value
5. Appreciative response.

And I allocate the statements as follows:

Categories				
1	*2*	*3*	*4*	*5*
a f g	**h**	**b c d j(1)**	**i**	**j(2) k**

Within the initial categories I couldn't classify statement **e.** But that's typical of what happens. It is not a 'one-off' process; as you get more data the possible category becomes more defined.

The next stage is to put together under each category heading the statements you've allocated. You do that in spreadsheet format – no room to show that here! But when you group the statements in this fashion you can start to see their meaning (and the limits of the categories). Organization is intellectually clarifying. Take category (3) above (occasionally useful). We get:

- sometimes I find something of interest – especially in catalogues: for the garden, things like that;

- it depends what it is;
- occasionally something attracts my attention;
- it's a mixture isn't it?

You may find that as the statements accumulate, the category is too big so that you need to subdivide; conversely you may decide to combine them. However, *many more statements don't add many more categories*. The typical range is not large and the first dozen or so questionnaires or recording schedules analysed will often account for three-quarters of the categories you'll end up with. In that sense it is not such a formidable task and, as you progress, you will come to know what to look for as well as how to go about it.

Now is the time when you'll appreciate the value of what was advised in Chapter 10, the 'piloting' chapter, that the analysis of the content of open questions cannot just wait until the main study has been completed. In particular that you have to judge whether the questions involved will make the task of analysis too difficult or time-consuming. But there is more to a trial exercise than that: you need to get the sense that you 'know how to do it'. A practice content analysis overcomes that concern; and having carried it out you will find you absorb the lessons over time.

15

Interpretation and Writing Up

We've analysed and organized our data (let us give ourselves the credit for being even-handed in that respect). But we still have to make sense of it in the form of an interpretive commentary, and indicate priorities for further research. This is a more personal and subjective business than is usually acknowledged.

The traditional conventions of academic writing obscure this subjectivity, for example by deleting references to self, the use of the passive voice and presenting the research process as more logical in order and operation than is in fact the case. But however objective a research report might appear, it was still written by someone with their own motivation and understanding; the 'logic' and 'objectivity' are a kind of formal cloak on the reality of the practice of research.

This is not an argument for self-indulgence in academic writing but for an open recording of the research process, from original conception to final (or interim) conclusions which make clear: *this is what I have done and how and why* – giving other people the chance to interrogate the researcher's procedures and 'findings'.

What is the purpose of research?

In the business of getting on and doing your research, submerged in the detail, it is possible to lose sight of where you are going or, indeed, that you are making (perhaps necessary) deviations in your route, if not your ultimate direction.

Research is not a predetermined process even if some textbooks, and the way academic papers are usually written, make it appear so. All social researchers are haunted by the ghost of scientific methodology: that research has to involve testing an *a priori* hypothesis (what you expect to find), usually expressed as a *null hypothesis* – i.e. that you will *not* find *x* or *y* (a difference between two groups given different treatments), one 'experimental', the other a 'control'.

Real-world social research doesn't work like that. There is a *purpose* – usually defined quite broadly – as in exploring attitudes to alternative medicine an example previously given; from which research *questions* emerge such as: *how do people come to take up alternative medicine?* By its very nature this approach is exploratory in character. In so far as a 'hypothesis' is concerned, it is hypothesis *seeking* rather than hypothesis testing. And, as you refine your methods, accumulate your data, so you develop your purpose and questions, particularly the latter. Research of any kind doesn't start out in a deliberate, tightly defined fashion: initially it is intuitive in character. Werner von Braun, the German rocket scientist, once said: 'Basic research is what I'm doing when I don't know what I'm doing'. Discoveries are made en route. It is more like a research journey than a research programme. The fact that fairly tight methods of data collection are employed (in this case, questionnaires and structured interviews) doesn't alter that fact; and the *process* of their development reflects how the tidier outcome is achieved.

This journey needs to be recorded and written up *as it happens*. It involves keeping a log of all those developments: the revisions, the insights, the influence of what you have read, your awareness of the limits of your methods and data. In other words, the research should be presented in such a way that the reader can follow in your footsteps. And from this faithfully recorded journey you can derive a logical and summary reconstruction that enables the reader to grasp quickly what you have been about. There is no contradiction here: they are complementary perspectives.

The importance of a summary

I once worked in a university department of psychology where there was an unwritten rule that PhD students should be ready to outline their research project to interested visitors, *in 5 minutes*. They did similar but longer presentations to others (peers, supervisors and so on). It did them a great deal of good even if they couldn't always see it at the time. Explaining to others, as teachers know, is an excellent way of understanding things better yourself.

If you cannot give a brief exposition of:

- the background to your research;
- what your purpose and questions were;
- what methods you used;
- what results you obtained;
- the meaning (explanation) of your findings;

then you are not yet in a position to write up. You cannot plunge into complex detail without some kind of simple map to guide you – which has to be in your head. And that, in turn, allows you to achieve a structure and organization within which you can incorporate the detail.

Presenting your findings

It is not difficult to appreciate that the development of your research project could be (and, perhaps, *should* be) presented as a chronological narrative, a kind of story. But the analogy also applies to how you present your results: your summary data with interwoven commentary and interpretation.

In Chapter 7 we emphasized the importance of putting

questions (and topics) into 'logical' developmental order so that one question leads into the next. As you write up your project, showing the pattern of answers to the questions, incorporating the results of tests of significance where appropriate, so your commentary becomes a narrative: linking and developing, referring back, anticipating what is to come. The task is to combine the reporting of your survey results with comment and interpretation so as to make maximum sense of your findings. Certainly over-interpretation must be avoided but distinctive features of the data can be highlighted, and the implications of what you have found marked out for further enquiry. *Unexpected* results can be emphasized in this fashion because they challenge preconceptions, and, in their turn, require to be explained.

The highly structured character of a questionnaire (and its interview variants) does provide the outline format for a research report. However, this is not an excuse for giving little more than a set of quantitative tables and figures, with the occasional element of statistical analysis. At each stage the question should be: what have I got to say about these results?

A practical example

For instance, taking Table 12.1 (p. 79) and the chi square 2×2 contingency table on p. 90 (Table 13.4), together with the original question and answer formats on pp. 39, we might write up as follows:

> The question relating to the Health Centre's appointment service, framed as a statement with which the respondents could agree or not was set out as follows:
>
> [We would insert from p. 39 here]
>
> Because we were interested in what was *wrong* with the appointments service we gave a choice of *two* negative answers, an in-between option (*not sure*) and only one positive choice. It was felt

that this would convey the message that we were interested in critical judgements particularly as it was followed by a request to *explain* why the respondent disagreed. [A content analysis of these responses is given in the next section.]

Table 12.1 from p. 79 gives the distribution of levels of agreement by age.

Several things are immediately apparent:
- younger people appear more likely to confirm that the appointments service is 'very good';
- older people appear more likely to disagree;
- the latter also appear more likely to be undecided.

How real are these apparent differences? If we disregard the 'not sure' group in Table 12.1 (because we only know that this reflects an inability or unwillingness to make a judgement) and combine the two 'disagree' categories, then we have a 2×2 contingency table which can be evaluated using chi square.

As we have calculated (p. 91) this produces a chi square of 4.35 which has a p value rather better than 0.05 (see table on p. 87) so it is clearly significant but not highly so.

From the perspective of a *qualitative* investigation we have two questions:

1. What are the kind of complaints made by the 'disagree' group?
2. Is there any difference in *kind* – as opposed to quantity – between the complaints made by older and younger patients?

We can see there is a difference statistically (because chi square has demonstrated this) but what does it mean?

Our next step is to carry out a content analysis of the responses of the two groups (45+ and under 45) to see whether there is a qualitative difference. [And so on; we explore this difference below.]

Analysing answers to open questions

We briefly covered the procedures for the categorical content analysis of open questions in the last chapter. Although they do not figure largely in survey questionnaires they are particularly challenging to write up. Let us consider the form of the data.

You have your 'substantive' statements listed under the category headings you have derived. In a written questionnaire the whole of the response is likely to be substantive because there will be less redundancy. There are two ways of presenting these statements:

- in a numerical table or bar graph (15 people made a statement which fitted this category, and so on);
- in the narrative write up, and under each category heading, presenting a selection from the *range* of statements within it: particularly those that say something a bit different.

To go back to the example in the previous section, the original question, framed as a statement was:

- The Health Centre provides a very good appointments service (TICK ONE BOX)
- ☐ agree
- ☐ not sure
- ☐ disagree
- ☐ strongly disagree

This was followed up by an opportunity to give reasons:

- If you have checked either **disagree** or **strongly disagree**, please say why:

_____

_____

_____

_____

A range of responses might look like the following:

a. It's difficult to get through before I leave for work and I can't phone later.
b. You often have to wait a long time if you want an appointment with a particular doctor.
c. It would be helpful if you could be told when it is a less busy time to ring.
d. The receptionist asks too many personal questions if you say it's urgent.
e. Often the phone just rings engaged.
f. A couple of times I've turned up for an appointment to be told they had no record of it.
g. The appointment time you're given is nothing like the time you're actually seen – difficult if you've taken time off work.
h. Evening surgery hours finish too early for many people who work full-time.
i. You have to make separate appointments to see a doctor and a practice nurse and they can't usually be fitted in at the same time – difficult for people who work.
j. When I've just called in to the surgery I've always been able to get an earlier appointment, I don't know why. It's a nuisance to have to do that.

From these we can derive possible category headings with statements located within them.

Table 15.1 Putting answers to open questions into categories

Category	Statement
Work-related problems	**a g h i**
Telephone contact	**c e**
Appointment delays/coordination	**b g i**
Reception efficiency/sensitivity	**d f j**

(*Note:* Some statements are allocated to more than one category because of overlap.)

You can see that categorization is a common sense business which enables you to point up areas needing attention (one purpose of a survey) and to link them together as different aspects of the same concern. You can also see that a simple open question like this, not particularly difficult to organize, nonetheless yields material that you wouldn't get by a precoded set of answers.

Weaving the statements into the narrative

With a small number of statements to classify, as in Table 15.1, presenting them in this format may be all that is necessary, together with a commentary which picks out particular features of the data. With a large number of statements it is a different matter. You can still construct a frequency table, either numerical or in the form of a bargraph. But with a hundred or more statements in some categories (as in a postal questionnaire) it becomes much more challenging.

However, the essential procedure is the same:

1. You identify substantive statements.
2. You derive categories (headings) from them and construct a spreadsheet.
3. You allocate statements to the categories on your spreadsheet.

If you are dealing with large numbers of statements you have to take the analysis a stage further, and continue as follows:

4. Group together very similar statements *within* the categories.
5. Identify key exemplar statements (the ones that say it best) from within these groupings.
6. Construct an appendix for these complete data sets which will be too bulky to go into the main text of a report.
7. Construct a table of exemplar quotations (indicating how many such quotations there are within each grouping).
8. Comment/discuss as you would with any other summary of this sort.

NB Since you can count the *frequencies* of quotations in particular categories chi square can be used here if markedly different patterns of response can be detected.

Discussion and discovery

In the main, the analysis, interpretation and discussion of your findings is done for the intended readership. You want them to understand and appreciate what you have been about and to learn from it. But this, sometimes laborious, process is one where you also clarify for yourself what you have been doing: itself a stage of discovery. These 'discoveries' need to be written up in your discussion, and the most important of them may be the questions raised: good research produces findings that point the way to further research. There are limits to what can be uncovered by survey methods which by their very nature can only provide a surface 'descriptive' account.

A survey may indicate areas or issues that require practical action (e.g. *We need to make our appointments system better suited to patients who work full-time*), or where supplementary qualitative exploratory research needs to be done (e.g. *What factors deter women from entering university civil engineering courses?*). In summary, what a social survey allows you to do is to describe an outline picture and highlight those features that warrant further attention.

But evaluating research is about more than evaluating the implications of the results. It is curious how following a very specific topic nonetheless throws up useful lessons about the business of research in general: that the main requirements are self-discipline, scrupulous attention to detail and the thoughtful justification of the project and the way it was carried out.

References

Bryman, A.* (1988) *Doing Research in Organizations*, London: Routledge.

Bryman, A (2001) *Social Research Methods*, Oxford: Oxford University Press.

Gillham, B. (2000) *The Research Interview*, London: Continuum.

Gillham. B.* (2000) *Case Study Research Methods*, London: Continuum.

Gillham, B.* (2005) *Research Interviewing: The Range of Techniques*, Maidenhead: Open University Press.

Glaser, B. G. and Strauss, A. L. (1967) *The Discovery of Grounded Theory: Strategies for Qualitative Research*, Chicago: Aldine.

Greene, J. and d'Oliviera, M. (1999) *Learning to Use Statistical Tests in Psychology*, Buckingham: Open University Press.

Halsey, A. H. and Webb, J. (2000) *Twentieth Century British Social Trends*, Oxford: Oxford University Press.

Moser, C. A. and Kalton, G.* (1986) *Survey Methods in Social Investigation*, Aldershot: Gower Publishing.

Office for National Statistics (2006) *British Crime Survey 2005*, London: ONS.

Office for National Statistics (2006) *General Household Survey 2005*, London: ONS.

Punch, K. F. (2003) *Survey Research: The Basics*, London: Sage Publications.

Robson, C. (1973) *Experiment, Design and Statistics in Psychology*, Harmondsworth: Penguin Books.

Robson, C. (1993) *Real World Research*, Oxford: Blackwell.

* = recommended further reading

Index

CPSIA information can be obtained
at www.ICGtesting.com
Printed in the USA
LVHW080527050319
609536LV00007B/95/P

9 780826 496300